pg. 101

S0-ERY-994

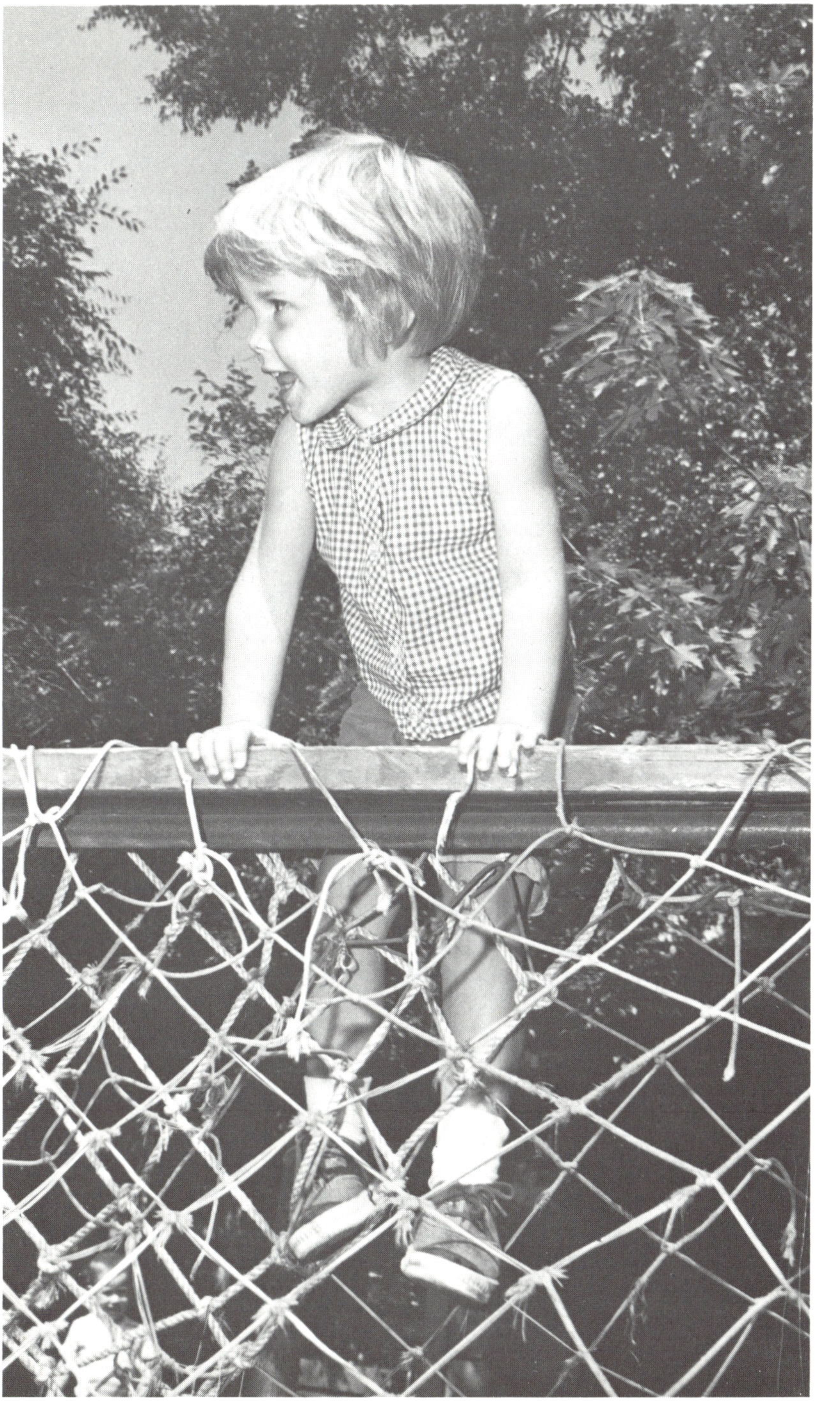

MOVEMENT OF THE YOUNG CHILD
AGES TWO TO SIX

Caroline B. Sinclair
*formerly Madison College and
research consultant
Richmond Public Schools*

Charles E. Merrill Publishing Company
A Bell & Howell Company
Columbus, Ohio

GV
443
.S48
1973

*Dedicated to
the fifty-seven young children
from whom I learned so much*

Published by
Charles E. Merrill Publishing Company
A Bell & Howell Company
Columbus, Ohio

Copyright© 1973 by Bell & Howell Company. All rights reserved. No part of this book may be reproduced in any form, electronic or mechanical, including photocopy, recording or any information storage and retrieval system, without permission in writing from the publisher.

International Standard Book Number: 0-675-08975-1

Library of Congress Catalog Card Number: 72-96100

1 2 3 4 5 6 7 8 9 10—77 76 75 74 73

Printed in the United States of America

PREFACE

This book is directed especially to teachers and parents and to others preparing to work with young children. It is designed to present information gained from four years of intensive research in the observation and analysis of the movement of preschool children and a lifetime of professional experience in physical education. It is intended to answer some of the questions now being asked about the development of young children—how they move, how they *should* move, what movement experiences we should provide for them.

The focus is upon the child and his developing abilities. Some knowledge of child psychology is a prerequisite for best understanding of this material. The use of the book as a text should be supplemented by observation and experience with children, by discussion and analysis, and by additional reading especially of cited authors. Local and state curriculum guides for preschool and kindergarten may also be used appropriately in supplement.

Illustrations have been chosen from real-life situations. The study of these photographs of young children in motion may be enhanced by observation of children and by use of films and slides.

Following an introductory chapter (one), chapter two describes fundamental motor tasks for young children and lists elements and standards for observation and appraisal. Chapters two through five present information on the typical movements and developing movement patterns of early childhood. Chapter six consists of a number of case studies for analysis and practice in problem solving. Chapters seven and eight deal with the essentials of the physical environment, the cooperative relationship of teacher and parent, and suggestions for developing a program of movement and integrating it into a broad and rich educational experience for young children.

The author acknowledges with gratitude the assistance given in the selection and use of photography by the staff of the Richmond City Schools (Mrs. Zelma T. Littlejohn), the American Association for Health, Physical Education, and Recreation (Mrs. Nancy Rosenberg), and the National Association for the Education of Young Children (Mrs. Georgianna Engstrom).

Appreciation is expressed to the many children who served as research subjects and to their parents and teachers; to the superintendent and staff of the Richmond Public Schools; to the director and staff of Belle Bryan Day Nursery, Richmond, Virginia; to the director and staff of the Division of Educational Research and Statistics of the Virginia State Department of Education, all of whom supported and endured the research; to Mrs. Betty Deal who typed and retyped the manuscript; and to the friends and colleagues whose interest and prodding inquiry have encouraged the preparation of this book.

C.B.S

CONTENTS

chapter one	MOVEMENT AS EDUCATION	1
chapter two	MOVEMENT TASKS	11
chapter three	THE DEVELOPMENT OF PATTERN IN MOVEMENT	31
chapter four	GENERAL CHARACTERISTICS OF MOVEMENT	41
chapter five	DIFFERENCES IN THE MOVEMENT OF CHILDREN	53
chapter six	CASE STUDIES	65
chapter seven	SPACE, TIME, AND EQUIPMENT	79
chapter eight	THE MOVEMENT PROGRAM	97
	APPENDIX	109

Contents

GLOSSARY	113
BIBLIOGRAPHY	117
INDEX	123

chapter one

MOVEMENT AS EDUCATION

This volume is devoted to the movement of young children. Its primary theses are 1) that movement is in itself educative (that learning occurs as one moves) and 2) that movement is essential to learning in early childhood.

The purpose of this chapter is to explore these two theses.

Proud parents, adoring grandparents, pediatricians, and psychologists have studied the developing movement of babies with great care. The Yale Clinic in a delightful film, *Posture and Locomotion* with narration by Arnold Gesell, has portrayed the usual sequence of this development from birth to eighteen months of age.[1] Others have, in general, substantiated the findings of Gesell and his associates presented in this film.

The motor development of infants has been assigned great importance in the study of human growth and development; it has been used as an index of the baby's intellectual, maturational, and social development; it has been assessed as an important factor in his health; in short it has been studied as, perhaps, the best indicator that all is

---

[1] Yale Clinic, *Posture and Locomotion* (Long Island City, New York: Instructional Sound Film, Erpi Classroom Films, Inc., 35-11 35th Street, 1934), 10 minutes, B/W.

2 Movement of the Young Child: Ages Two to Six

right—or wrong—in his world. Yet surprisingly little attention has been paid to the child's movement between infancy and school age. An era of concern appeared in the 1930s and early 1940s when Nancy Bayley,[2] Mary Gutteridge,[3] F.L. Goodenough,[4] and others conducted research and published their findings, but as late as 1960 Ruth Glassow[5] commented on the dearth of information on gross movements of young children, other than early locomotion.

Within the last few years new interests and theories in the education of the preschooler, the handicapped child, and the underachiever have focused on movement, and especially on movement as a learning experience.

No one questions the importance of the ability to move as a precious asset; for children, especially, movement has both quantitative and qualitative values. To move is essential to life itself; to move often and vigorously is a priority for growth and development of the body and all its parts; exercise is one of the vital pacemakers for health; to move *well* gives qualitative value to life. Joy in movement is one of the biggest and best reasons for experiencing it. Moreover, movement is a means of communication and of creative expression.

Physical exercise is a stabilizer of body chemistry and through the minimizing of stress factors plays a significant role in mental and emotional health. Through movement a child experiences both self-mastery and mastery of his environment and thus builds a positive self-image.

Movement is a learning experience and thus is of great concern to education. In the further development of this thought five points will be considered:

1. Movement is in itself a perceptual experience.
2. The nervous system obeys the physiological law of use.
3. The body's input and output systems are interdependent.
4. Maturation and learning are both aspects of the process of growth.
5. Movement is one of the essential tool subjects.

---

[2] Nancy Bayley, "The Development of Motor Abilities During The First Three Years," *Monograph of the Society for Research in Child Development*, vol. 1, (Washington, D.C.: 1935), 1-26.

[3] Mary V. Gutteridge, "A Study of Motor Achievements of Young Children," *Archives of Psychology*, No. 244 (New York: Columbia University, 1939), 178 pp.

[4] F.L. Goodenough and R.C. Smart, "Interrelationships of Motor Abilities in Young Children," *Child Development* 6 (1935): 1-153.

[5] Ruth B. Glassow, "Motor Development" in *Encyclopedia of Educational Research*, ed. Chester W. Harris, 3rd ed., (New York: Macmillan Co., 1960), p. 901.

MOVEMENT AS A PERCEPTUAL EXPERIENCE

In addition to the historic five senses (sight, hearing, taste, smell and touch—sometimes referred to as the exteroceptors) there is now an awareness of the proprioceptors—so named because organs are placed *deep* beneath the exterior surfaces of the body. Through these one is able to experience sensations of position, movement, and equilibrium; other sense organs are also assisted or augmented by the proprioceptors —particularly those of pain, pressure, sight, and hearing.

The proprioceptor most acutely concerned with equilibrium is located in the vestibular apparatus of the inner ear. Other proprioceptors which must function in close association with the vestibular organs are the muscle spindles, the Golgi tendon organs, and the joint receptors; these have often been referred to collectively as the organs of "muscle sense" or kinesthesis. They are located in the skeletal muscle tissue and in tendons and joints of the body. They enable one to know the position of the body and its parts in space, to recognize movement of the body and its parts and the direction and speed of these movements, and to experience muscle tension or lack of it.

The receptors in the muscles, tendons, and joints are activated whenever movement occurs, and they are doubtless functioning before birth. They are thought to constitute the earliest input system of the body. This sensory-motor mechanism, activated through movement, thus provides the first learning or experience system and is of prime importance in maturation and growth during infancy and early childhood.

Movement itself is change. During movement a constant feedback is supplied making appraisal and adjustment possible, or even necessary, in a continuum which leads eventually to skilled movement of a remarkable complexity, to refinement, and to support and involvement of other sensory pathways and of all areas of the neural system.

THE NERVOUS SYSTEM AND THE PHYSIOLOGICAL LAW OF USE

A machine or other inanimate body which is used wears out. The human body develops and grows through use and this is known as the physiological law of use. The body has its own built-in system of growth, repair, and even of spare parts. But growth and renewal are available only *on demand.* Muscles grow big and strong in use, but develop atrophy in disuse. The importance of exercise for organic health is well established. Fernand La Grange wrote in 1890 that running creates much work for the heart and lungs, and truly the demands of vigorous exercise are the best developer of the vital organs.[6] As demands increase, new capillary growth extends in a greater network and, in the lungs, tiny alveoli open and begin to function.

In education, in psychology, and in medicine some effort has been made to apply the law of use to the nervous system. Its applicability is currently supported by observation of behavior and clinical experience but conclusive physiological evidence has not yet been obtained. The theory is this: the nervous system, including the brain and its cortex, obeys the law of use. Only as it is used will its potential for use be developed. In the human infant much of the potential lies dormant at birth. As the child grows in size, stature, and ability so the neurones grow in myelinization, length of fiber, complexity and strength of synaptic association. Within the brain there are known to be millions of cells which can serve as spare parts should an area of the brain be damaged. These cells represent potential for learning, for storage of information, and for the integration and use of knowledge far beyond the intellectual levels which man has yet achieved.

And, according to the law of use, the key to this potential is demand. In basic military training a man is expected to triple the strength of his arms and shoulder girdle in eight weeks. How to accomplish this is well established. However, we do not yet know as well how to tap the reserves of the brain. There is considerable evidence to show that the nervous system, like the circulatory, the respiratory, and the muscular systems, responds to demand and that, in early childhood, the muscular system is a natural and ready partner for nervous system development.

THE BODY'S INPUT AND OUTPUT SYSTEMS AS INTERDEPENDENT

The nervous system and the muscles of the body are singularly dependent upon each other constituting a stimulus-response mechanism in which neither can function without the other. A muscle must receive a nerve impulse in order to contract; a motor nerve has no function without motor response and even a sensory nerve falls short of its goal if it cannot elicit a response to its input.

The feedback mechanism described so clearly by Elizabeth Gardner gives assurance that small nerve fibers are monitoring every movement,

---

[6] Fernand La Grange, *Physiology of Bodily Exercise* (New York: D. Appleton and Company, 1890), p. 82 et seq.

providing proprioceptive and exteroceptive information so that awareness, assessment, and modification may take place instantly.[7] In short, input (sensory) not only activates output (motor) but accompanies it and even derives from it; therefore, the two are inseparable in the study of motor learning (all learning in fact). For as the learner participates in a new, or even a familiar, experience he receives sensations from it; he then perceives and interprets these sensations, modifies his responses because of them and climbs to a higher level of achievement. Thus he becomes ready for new learning experiences.

Research has identified the mechanisms through which the "feedback" of the neuromuscular system occurs (the three types of proprioceptors, the short and long motor fibers, the synapses in both the central and autonomic nervous systems, the specific tracts of the central nervous systems). In practical application and in clinical situations better motor performance is obtained by carefully directing "input"; likewise better learning follows or perhaps results from heightened motor experience. This is Dewey's theory of "learning by doing" also espoused by Pestalozzi, Montessori, Piaget, and other great educators throughout the ages. In all situations, however, and in the consideration of any child it is well to recognize the complexity of human nature and the diversity of human personality. Not only is each person different genetically but he aspires to, selects from, compensates for, focuses on, relates to, and integrates information in a way which is uniquely his own *today*—and it may indeed be different tomorrow!

To repeat—input and output are interdependent and together provide experience and, from this, *learning. Neurological organization* is the term now often used in reference to the growth and maturation of the nervous system. It implies improved utilization of all parts of the central and autonomic nervous systems and includes increased myelinization, nerve fiber growth and repair, more extensive use of brain cells, increased synaptic efficiency for response and/or inhibition, and other factors. According to present knowledge it does *not* imply an increase in the number of nerve cells (neurones); the number of these is believed to be complete at birth and one lost cannot be replaced except by substitution. Fortunately the human body is equipped with so many neurones especially within the brain that an almost infinite number of "spare parts" is provided.

---

[7] Elizabeth B. Gardner, "Proprioceptive Reflexes and Their Participation in Motor Skills," *Quest*, Monograph XII (May 1969), pp. 1-25.

MATURATION AND LEARNING AS ASPECTS OF THE PROCESS OF GROWTH

Maturation is heredity at work given the nourishment of a suitable and stimulating environment, while learning is the interaction of heredity and action (or response) so that after each response the individual is able to perform at a higher level.

Just as lower forms of life have inborn time systems which control their lives so also does man. In his life span there is a right time for many experiences; there is an ordered sequence in his growth. Educators need to know the order, timing, and sequences of growth so that they may provide the right experiences at the right time.

George Sage after a careful review of studies of infants lists the intermediate steps to standing erect and walking as: kicking the legs, rolling, hitching (locomotion in a sitting position), crawling, creeping, standing with support, and finally walking without support.[8] By fourteen months most babies will walk without support, some will take longer, and walking or not, they will "mix and match" the intermediate steps in a variety of patterns and sequences, for even at this age each is an individual and his behavior is unique to himself.

Such detailed study has been lacking for the child who is past infancy but not yet in school. A.L. Gesell,[9] Myrtle McGraw[10] and others have made notable contributions to the study of motor development in early childhood and more recently R.L. Wickstrom[11] has studied the developing movement pattern in six activities and has included young children in the continuum.

A longitudinal study of children two, three, and four years of age was started by this author in 1966 and completed in 1970.[12] The findings indicated most children acquire reasonable proficiency in a large number of motor tasks (fundamental movements) by age five and that the ability to perform these tasks appears either progressively over a period of time or "in toto" at a rather specific time, if the child is provided with appropriate opportunities. Some encouragement was pro-

---

[8] George H. Sage, *Introduction to Motor Behavior* (Reading, Mass.: Addison Wesley Publishing Co., 1971), p. 434.

[9] Arnold L. Gesell and H. Thompson, "Learning and Growth in Identical Infant Twins: An Experimental Study of the Method of Co-Twin Control," *Genetic Psychological* Monograph VI (1929), pp. 1-124.

[10] Myrtle B. McGraw, *The Neuromuscular Maturation of the Human Infant*, reprint edition 1963-1966 (New York: Hafner Publishing Co., 1966), pp. 1-140.

[11] Ralph L. Wickstrom, *Fundamental Motor Patterns* (Philadelphia: Lea and Febiger, 1970), pp. 1-178.

[12] Caroline B. Sinclair, *Movement and Movement Patterns* (Richmond, Va.: Division of Educational Research and Statistics, State Department of Education, 1971), pp. 1-24.

vided by the researcher but little motivation was necessary for at all ages studied the children reveled in movement and seemed to experience much satisfaction from both the effort and the achievement. The findings reveal that there are periods of readiness when the prerequisite maturation has occurred and the child will learn a given motor task with great facility. Although children are indeed different the age at which this readiness occurred and the patterns of movement in which it was manifested were amazingly similar. For example, the two year old could walk and jump from both feet, but he was unwilling to stand on one foot or to try to hop; he was inept in taking off from both feet unless his stance was from a chair or other elevation. At three he could take off from a mark or flat surface and would try to hop but with little success and on only one foot. By 4½ he could hop on one foot and would attempt it with limited success on the other.

Thus it may be concluded that the simple common movements of locomotion (walking, running, jumping, hopping, skipping, etc.), of throwing and striking, of pushing and pulling, of creeping and climbing, which are the bases of our physical work and play have a genetic foundation built into the neuromuscular system. This foundation is activated by the growth processes and by the individual's responses to his environment—in short, maturation is of great significance in the movement of the young child even though it must be reinforced by timely provision of opportunity and encouragement. The findings here referred to will be presented in detail in chapters two, three, four, five, and six.

MOVEMENT AS AN ESSENTIAL TOOL SUBJECT

Movement is a tool subject because like the three Rs it opens so many doors to learning and it is essential because without movement it is doubtful that any learning could occur at all.

In the act of moving a child learns to move and, hopefully, to move well. This in itself is a desirable objective of education. But through moving he becomes involved with the world about him and learns of it; he enhances his perceptions and broadens his interpretations; his life becomes enriched and many doors are opened to him.

Other tool subjects are dependent on movement; one cannot read or write and can be greatly inhibited in mathematics if he has not mastered small and intricate movements of hand and eye. But movement, gross movement, is a medium for learning also. How better to learn dimensions than to explore them in a crib, a playpen, a room, or a yard? What is *up* if it is not rising to one's feet or climbing up a lad-

8 Movement of the Young Child: Ages Two to Six

der or stairway? What is *weight* if it is not lifted or carried? What is *gravity* if one were to fall "up" and not "down"? How can *skipping* be learned except by skipping? Or *swimming* be experienced except by swimming? And what of the concommitant learnings about water, wetness, resistance, breathing, and rhythm?

As in teaching other tool subjects, both methods and activities for teaching movement must be progressive and arranged in orderly sequence.

Basic, fundamental movements are of first concern—locomotion in many forms, movement experiences with many and diverse objects, suspension, traveling through space, receiving and imparting force, maneuvering the body as a whole. As a child learning to read must confront words, phrases, and sentences in different contexts so must the child learning to move use the fundamentals in a variety of ways, for different purposes and in diverse situations. Only then does he learn to deal with abstractions of space, time, and direction; thus too he gains a concept of himself, his structure, his ability to live in and master his environment and his relationship to it. "Look at me!" is the gleeful cry of the child who climbs to the top of the ladder, jumps over the bar, or "skins the cat" on the tree limb or acting bar.

Within these fundamentals teachers must learn to look for and recognize developing qualities of opposition, weight transfer, momentum, acceleration, synchrony, symmetry, balance, rhythm, laterality, and perceptual control (not only of sight, but also of muscle sense, of hearing, and of equilibrium).

A child who is able to read likes to read. A child who has learned to sing enjoys singing. A child *can* move and normally he wants to move. As he becomes proficient in more movement skills he wants to use them. For the young child just to perform is enough—to run, to climb, to throw, to jump; but even at ages three and four and certainly at five and six he needs, at least sometimes, a goal—to run *to* something, to jump *over* something, to climb to the top! And each new situation, each piece of equipment, each toy, each new arrangement of the familiar objects presents a challenge to the small child.

Soon these are not enough and the curriculum in movement must provide ever increasing challenges in which these skills are used in complex combinations, intricate refinements, competition, daring strategy, creative expression, adventurous exploration, satisfying rhythm, and culturally developed and established forms such as games and dances. Each of these places additional demands upon the child, each involves perceptual experience, and each calls for decision making. And as the child meets each new demand, he grows and learns and thus goes on to higher levels of challenge and learning.

What a big world of exploration is opened up for the child when he becomes self-moving! And how this is enhanced when he can run, climb, swim, and ride a bicycle or horse! And how fascinating and fruitful to discover that balls are to be thrown, hoops to be rolled, ropes to be jumped, and that these and many other objects can be moved and used in a great variety of ways all to one's own purpose!

And how exciting and gratifying is the self-discovery that is gained through movement—to realize that *I* can go from here to there—and that *I* can go much faster on skates or on a bike! To recognize the control that *I* have over the world around me because I can move the objects in it! To feel that *I* am different when I move this way or that and that *I* can produce a mood or say something by the way I move! To move with other people and to find that this has special significance —I can help or I can hinder; I can oppose or I can support; I can relate or I can remain aloof.

And so the child learns through movement—and by movement— about the world around him, about himself, about other people; he learns to move and with this tool he is helped to acquire other learning tools.

SUMMARY

The young child lives in a world in which his movement is paramount. Through it he achieves, explores, communicates, expresses himself, grows, and learns. As he grows in strength and skill and as perception develops he is constantly responding to the world about him and through each response he learns—and thus becomes capable of more learning.

The problem is to present the child with the best developmental and learning opportunities *at the right time* and in the *proper sequence.* Among these learning experiences movement is important both for its own sake and as a stimulant for neurological development and growth. In the latter function, it not only places kinesthetic demands upon the nervous system but it supports and helps to make possible other sensory functions such as *sight* (movement of the head and eyes), *hearing* (movement and support of the head), and *taste* (in movement of the tongue). Pediatricians, neurologists, psychologists, optometrists, teachers, and students in the fields of special education, remedial reading, speech pathology, and rehabilitation are among those who give credence to this theory and whose research is bringing new knowledge to support and develop it.

Keturah Whitehurst summarized a beautifully expressed address on what movement means to a young child:

10   Movement of the Young Child: Ages Two to Six

It means life; self-discovery; environmental discovery, both physical and social; freedom, both spatial and self expressive; safety; communication; enjoyment and sensuous pleasure; acceptance.[13]

Thus she also has emphasized the importance of movement *as* and *in* education and her points enhance and support the statements that:

1. Movement is in itself a perceptual experience.
2. The nervous system obeys the physiological law of use.
3. The body's input and output are interdependent.
4. Maturation and learning are both aspects of the process of growth.
5. Movement is one of the essential tool subjects.

And these statements give further credence to the theses that *movement is in itself educative* and *movement is essential to learning in early childhood.*

References

Cratty, Bryant J. *Active Learning.* Englewood, New Jersey: Prentice-Hall, Inc., 1971

Flavell, J.H. *The Developmental Psychology of Jean Piaget.* Princeton, New Jersey: Van Nostrand Co., Inc., 1963.

Gitter, Lena L. *The Montessori Way.* Seattle, Washington: Special Child Publications, 1970.

Metheney, Eleanor. "Moving and Learning." In *Virginia Conference on Movement Experiences for Young Children,* edited by Eleanor Bobbitt. Farmville, Va.: Longwood College, 1971.

Sinclair, Caroline. "Movement Experiences for Young Children." In *Working Conference Proceedings,* Virginia Conference on Movement Experiences for Young Children, edited by Eleanor Bobbitt. Farmville, Va.: Longwood College, 1970.

Whitehurst, Keturah E. "The Young Child—What Movement Means to Him." *The Significance of the Young Child's Motor Development,* pp. 51-55, Washington, D.C.: National Association for the Education of Young Children, 1971.

---

[13] Keturah E. Whitehurst, "The Young Child: What Movement Means to Him," *The Significance of the Young Child's Motor Development* (Washington, D.C., National Association for the Education of Young Children, 1971), p. 55.

chapter two

MOVEMENT TASKS

Young children—perhaps all children—enjoy movement for movement's sake; they are also extremely purposeful about their movement. The author selected twenty-five movement tasks which included those movements considered as fundamental or basic to the complex motor activities of work, play, and the movement arts. At least two of these were added for specific purposes: ball bouncing to offer challenge in ball handling and eye-hand efficiency, and the figure-8-run to challenge agility with varied changes of direction and to give opportunity for motor planning (to visualize or project a sequence of movements before carrying them out). The equipment needed for the tasks is relatively simple. These twenty-five motor tasks, in combination and with variations, are sufficient to constitute a good movement curriculum for the early childhood years but certainly there are other motor activities that may also be used advantageously.

Persons who work with small children should be able to present simple motor tasks in ways which will interest the children and enable them to achieve as quickly and easily as possible. Educators must be able to vary or change a task so that challenge is always provided. They must be able to distinguish between good and poor movement and know how to help the child to improve. To help teachers *observe*,

12   Movement of the Young Child: Ages Two to Six

to help them know what to look for and how to judge success and improvement, each task is listed here with its primary elements, and suggestions are given for judging achievement. The age of average expectancy is also indicated.

In judging a child's achievement one must remember that his goal may not be that of the teacher and that small units of improvement may be as significant or even more so than larger units.

The movement tasks are presented in alphabetical order for easy reference; significant elements are listed; standards are given for success and basic pattern, and ages of expectancy for these are noted. Ages at which success and basic pattern may be expected are summarized in Table I (See p. 29).

1. *Ascending stairs*   This is an important activity for many children and a ready challenge for those unfamiliar with stairways.

Elements to be observed include: Advancing foot over foot (instead of foot to foot on each step); opposition (right hand and left foot move forward together and vice versa); no support (wall or hand rail not used unless needed for safety); body faces forward (if stair rise is high children may turn to side); climbs in a straight line (indicative of good balance); movements are even and rhythmic; body is well aligned.

Achievement may be judged by *success* (ascends without resorting to all fours), usually attained by age 2, and by the degree to which the elements listed are demonstrated. The key feature in arriving at a *basic pattern* in the performance of this task appears to be advancing foot over foot which is usually started at the age of 3 or soon thereafter. Stairs should be of appropriate dimensions for small children.

2. *Bouncing on the bounce board*   (See Appendix, p. 108 for specifications of this equipment.) This activity is especially zestful for children; the rhythm appears to be both enjoyable and soothing; the task requires controlled use of all parts of the body and leads to awareness of the body parts; a deviation in the use of hand, foot, or head brings quick results and leads to awareness of direction and laterality.

Elements are: Maintenance of balance (does not fall down or off); bounces four or more times successively; uses arms in elevation (above shoulders); uses ankles in both flexion (when landing and following board down) and extension (in propelling body upward); increases height gradually; arms pause at or above shoulder level (to time with greater height); rhythmic and even movements.

Achievement may be judged by *success* (four or more successive bounces without help) usually attained at age 2½. A very young child

When bouncing on a board, bedsprings, or trampoline
ankle extension is used in varying degrees.

or one who is fearful should be held by one or both hands until he gains a little confidence; this practice should *not* be continued as he will depend upon it, lean forward, and fail to achieve a balanced position. The child should place himself in the middle of the board for best success. Achievement is also represented in the degree to which the child demonstrates the other elements. The key feature in achieving *basic pattern* seems to be using the arms to lead the bounce and timing in holding the arms elevated to the point of greatest height of the bounce; the basic pattern may be expected at age 4½.

3. *Bouncing a large ball* The ball should be no larger than a soccer or volley ball but larger than a softball; it should of course be inflated and may be of rubber or plastic. The child should move with the ball for best control and for flexible use.

Elements are: Starts with both hands (this is usual but not essential); uses one hand (may change from right to left and vice versa but seldom does unless encouraged); uses knee to waist height (for best control); moves at moderate speed; moves with ball; covers space.

Achievement may be judged by *success* (suggested standard is control of ball for four or more successive bounces), usually reached at age 4½, and by the elements demonstrated. A *basic pattern* has been developed when the child is able to do six successive bounces when covering space at a walk or four when covering space at a run; this may be expected at age 5½.

4. *Carrying* Equipment used for this activity should be varied in accordance to the age, size, and strength of the child. A small suitcase-type bag may be used; it must be strongly made. The following weights are suggested:

    For the two year old — 8 pounds
    For the three year old —10 pounds
    For the four year old —12 pounds
    For the five year old —16 pounds
    For the six year old —20 pounds

Of course children may and should lift and carry many objects of varying sizes, shapes, and weights. In this task the picking up and the putting down are as significant as the carrying and should be observed.

Elements are: Bends knees to pick up weight; keeps object close to body; supports weight off floor the full distance (15-20 feet); holds

Small children usually flex the knees and hips when lifting.

trunk erect except in sideward compensation for weight; moves in a direct path; moves at a steady pace; controls weight in putting down (does not let it drop); uses one hand (for suitcase carrier).

Achievement may be judged by *success* (supports weight for the entire distance), which is achieved at age 2 and thereafter, and by demonstration of the listed elements. Carrying with one hand with control of the body alignment and balance is considered indicative of *basic pattern*. Young children are persistent in their efforts to carry or move heavy objects and usually achieve basic pattern at age 2. The tasks and tools given them should be challenging but within the limits of their strength.

5. *Catching a ball* The ball for younger children should be large and soft, but no larger than a soccer or volley ball. At age 5 a smaller ball such as a tennis ball may be substituted; many tennis clubs, colleges, and high schools will gladly contribute used tennis balls in quantity so that each child may have one or the children may work in couples. For the very young children, and on some occasions for others, bean bags may be more useful than balls. Ball handling is important in the play culture of all nations. It is helpful in learning about distance, direction, and force. It is conducive to the development of flexibility and strength in hands and wrists. Catching of thrown balls should be preceded by playing with rolling and self-thrown balls, bean bags, and sponge balls.

Elements are: Hands are placed in readiness; one foot is advanced in readiness or an adjustment of the feet is made to this stance as the ball is received; uses two hands, advances to the use of one primarily for small ball; eyes are open and focus on ball; "gives" (slight backward movement) to lessen impact; uses reaction of catch (the "give") to start return throw.

Achievement is dependent upon the way in which the ball is thrown so it is important that the throw be adjusted to the child's skill. The ball should be thrown lightly from a short distance; for very young children the thrower should stand at about six feet and toss the ball very gently into the child's hands and arms so that the catch is almost passive; as he responds the distance and force of the throw should be increased; the ball should reach the child at low-chest (just above the waist) height. The child may be considered *successful* if he catches two of three well-thrown balls which is usually done at age 2½ and progress is also exhibited by the use of the elements named. The *basic* catching *pattern* is indicated when the child uses his hands actively in catching (does not cradle the ball in his arms unless thrown with great force), and this pattern appears only irregularly in early childhood.

16 Movement of the Young Child: Ages Two to Six

6. *Climbing a ladder or ladder-like structure*   Climbing is essentially an all-fours (both hands and both feet) movement and the young child moves easily from creeping to climbing. He likes to climb because it gives him a new perspective on the world and places him on a level with or above the adults about him. A small child seldom exhibits fear of height in climbing unless he has learned to be fearful through overprotection or accident. Equipment must be sturdy and supervision is essential. Climbing is a vigorous activity and much needed for young children because it develops the muscles of the trunk and limbs thus demanding similar development of heart and lungs; also it is conducive to simultaneous and oppositional use of the limbs thus fostering development of the nervous system.

Elements are: Uses arms in alternation; uses foot-over-foot action; uses opposition; body faces ladder; climbs to the designated point (top if practicable); movements are steady and rhythmic.

In climbing this inclined ladder both children are using opposite hand and foot with the hand slightly preceding the foot.
Photograph by Donna J. Harris, The Merrill Palmer Institute Detroit, Michigan

Achievement may be judged by *success* in reaching the top (or designated point), usually achieved at age 2½, and by demonstration of the elements listed. The *basic pattern* is indicated by foot-over-foot progression when the distance between rungs of the ladder is not too great for the child to reach easily; this is usually attained at age 4.

7. *Creeping* This is the child's first really efficient locomotion and he should be encouraged to achieve a high level of proficiency. Like climbing it is highly developmental and can be used with safety and enjoyment. It is a useful tool for exploration and enlarges learning opportunities. Children who have not already achieved opposition (movement of opposite hand and foot simultaneously) in creeping should be given much practice even at ages 4, 5, and later.

Elements are: Uses arms alternately; uses legs alternately; uses limbs in opposition; points hands forward; keeps feet off the floor when moving knees forward; keeps back level; controls direction.

Achievement may be judged by *success* (covers designated distance on hands and knees—or feet), usually attained at age 2 or earlier, and by the degree to which the elements are demonstrated. *Basic pattern*

In creeping on a stable or moving surface children usually demonstrate hand-foot opposition.

is indicated by the use of opposition and smooth, rhythmic progression and is usually demonstrated at age 2½ or 3.

8. *Descending stairs*   Going down stairs in an erect, rhythmic fashion is much more demanding than going upstairs; it is also more hazardous.

Elements are: Foot-over-foot action; uses no support; body faces forward; arms used for balance; arms used in opposition (this also is for balance but is a later development than arms held sideward); descends in straight line; rhythmic, even movement; body well aligned.

Achievement may be judged by *success* (descends in erect position without help), usually reached at age 2½, and by the use of the elements listed. *Basic pattern* is achieved when progression is foot-over-foot with no marked deviation in rhythm—may be expected at age 4.

9. *Figure-8-run*   For detailed description of this task see Appendix, p. 109. It requires the child to follow a prescribed course while running and involves a number of changes of direction around designated objects.

Elements include: Starts promptly on signal; turns first to own right; alternates direction of turns; maintains balance; maintains speed; turns close to obstacles; uses arms for balance; follows course; shows evidence of motor planning.

Achievement may be judged by *success* (covers the course in any order), usually attained at age 5½, and by the extent to which the elements are demonstrated. *Basic pattern* is indicated when the child completes the circuit with one or more crossovers and maintains balance and speed; this standard is suggested as a criterion but will seldom be reached until age 6 or later. The motor planning required is demanding for preschool children and not really essential in basic movement pattern. As a motor task the figure-8-run is appropriate at ages 4 and 5 and may be simplified for younger children.

10. *Forward roll*   Although small children learn this activity very easily a minimum of instruction is recommended, for, at first trial, many children will hold the neck stiff and thereby experience some discomfort. A small mat, rug, or pad should be used. The child squats at the edge of the mat, the teacher tells him to tuck his head (and places one hand on the back of the child's head to hold it tucked) and the child rolls, the teacher assisting as necessary. After one or two tries the child is usually successful; if not, the teacher should continue assisting as needed. The forward roll is conducive to agility (body maneuverability), has high safety value (in falls), is basic to all gymnastics, and has great value for orientation in space. The child who learns it early and goes on to related use of it is fortunate indeed.

Elements are: Hands pointed ahead; uses hands for partial support; tucks head; rounds back; flexes knees and hips; rolls straight; comes to feet from roll. Note that these elements apply to the roll in a tuck position; the pike position is also quite acceptable and some children will use it; in this position the knees are straight, the hips high, *but the head is tucked.*

Achievement is indicated by *success* (the child rolls over), usually experienced at age 2½, and by the use of the elements listed. *Basic pattern* is acquired when the child rolls over with head tucked and back rounded and may be expected with some inconsistency at age 5.

11. *Galloping* A locomotor activity in which the individual moves forward leading with one foot (right or left) bringing the other up to it in an uneven, two-beat rhythmic pattern. Young children, if encouraged, will usually gallop before they skip or slide. The gallop is learned most easily by exposure to "galloping" music or percussion (drum, hand claps, etc.).

Elements are: One foot leads; body faces forward; can lead with either foot; rhythmic and steady; uses arms in balance; staccato movement.

Achievement is indicated by success (maintains an identifiable gallop), usually at age 2, and by demonstration of the elements listed. The *basic pattern* is attained when the gallop is demonstrated with steady rhythm and this may be expected at age 4. Most children will gallop with preferred foot leading (preference for right or left seems to be evenly divided) long before they are able to do so comfortably with the "other" foot leading. Both leads can be used well by most children at 4½.

12. *Hanging* A tiny infant can support his weight when grasping a bar with his hands; so also can most young children for as long as four seconds or more. Some are fearful and some will have to be assisted in starting and getting down. The height of the bar should be just beyond the child's reach when he is standing below it but a bar placed at a greater height can be used. The leader should provide a landing mat or other soft surface for landing if the distance is more than eighteen inches (less for very small children). In timing count the seconds aloud so that the child may participate also.

Elements are: Assumes position without help; uses overgrasp (children will generally use an overgrasp although the undergrasp is thought to have some mechanical advantages); holds position four to twenty seconds; head and shoulders in normal position (in so-called passive hanging the shoulders ride up toward the ears, the scapulae are well

20   Movement of the Young Child: Ages Two to Six

separated, and the chest may be low with the head forward); arms are straight; gets down without help.

Achievement is recognized by *success* (support of weight by hands in hanging position at least four seconds), which may be expected at age 2½, and by use of the elements listed. *Basic pattern* may be considered achieved if the child can hold the position for ten seconds. This is usual at age 4.

At two and older the child is well able to support his own weight when grasping a bar.
Photograph by Verna M. Fausey, Nashville, Tennessee

13. *Hitting*   There are many kinds of hitting and striking motions. The motor task selected was that of hitting a tennis ball from a batting tee with a bat of appropriate size and weight. Some children are content to move the ball from the tee; others wish to emulate the baseball players they see on TV. In order to elicit the elements of basic pattern and more mature performance, encourage the child to hit *hard*.

Elements are: Making contact with the ball; sideward stance; shifting weight (away from ball) in preparation;° shifting weight in hitting°

(forward or toward the line of flight); use of body rotation;° control of direction of ball; follows through° (continues movement of body and/or bat after hitting); contacts ball squarely; hits right to left (this is usual but some children will normally hit left to right); uses both hands on bat.

Achievement is indicated by *success* (at least one contact in three trials), which is irregular at age 2 and thereafter, and by use of the elements listed; hitting from a tee is very satisfying to young children but since their eye-hand efficiency is low they should have many other striking tasks; the tees may be adjusted to use larger balls. *Basic pattern* is demonstrated when the child utilizes at least three of the four elements starred (°) as these indicate a real transfer of weight and the coordinated use of body parts (total body assembly), the basic pattern is demonstrated infrequently at the ages studied.

At three boys are more likely to assume a good batting stance than girls; this left-handed batter exhibits some body rotation.
Photograph by Orville Andrews, Cupertino, California

14. *Hopping* This is a locomotor activity which appears significant in the achievement of balance; one foot is suspended in air while the individual moves by taking off and landing on the other.

Elements are: Hops successively (four times or more); hops in straight line; hops on preferred foot; holds free foot up to rear; uses arms for balance; hops on nonpreferred (other) foot.

Achievement consists of *success* (four or more successive hops), usually reached at age 4, and demonstration of the elements listed. *Basic pattern* is acquired when the child can accomplish at least four successive hops on the preferred foot and holds the free foot up and to the rear; this pattern is common at age 4½.

15. *Kicking* This task varies in method and uses. A soccer ball or playground ball 6-8 inches in diameter may be used; it should be rather soft. It should be placed for the younger children and rolled to those 4 years or older.

Elements are: Moves toward the ball; contacts ball with foot; times back swing for kick; uses limbs in opposition (if the ball rises sharply both arms will rise to or above shoulder level to maintain balance; if the ball travels forward with mild upward inclination the opposite arm will usually move forward with the kicking foot); uses same foot in each trial; extends knee in kicking; contacts ball squarely; controls direction; moves in direction of kicked ball (follow-through).

Achievement is indicated by *success* (ball is kicked forward its full circumference or more), usually attained at age 2, and by demonstration of the elements listed. *Basic pattern* is apparent when the child kicks the ball from a back swing or in the stride of a run either with the arms moving forward-sideward or in opposition; it may be expected frequently but irregularly at age 4 and thereafter.

16. *Pulling* Many objects may be pulled and pushed; in order to make the task more consistent, a small bench was used and a rider was provided matched to the size and weight of the child pulling (see Appendix p. 110). Children use varied methods for accomplishing this task; the elements listed are those most often used successfully.

Elements are: Moves obstacle the full distance (4-6 feet); hands placed in "pull" position (grasping sides of bench at end); exerts force in line with resistance; keeps contact with object; applies force steadily after starting; controls direction; uses long, open stance at start; adjusts body to resistance.

Achievement is attained with *success* (moves obstacle—bench with rider—full distance), usually at age 2, and with the use of the elements listed. *Basic pattern* is denoted by success with appropriate body adjustment (body may be lowered to approach the line of resistance); adjustment is inappropriate when body parts are not in harmony or resist each other. Basic pattern may be expected at age 4.

Movement Tasks 23

The girl on the stump has stabilized herself for
the forceful effort necessary in assisting her playmate.
Photograph by Philipp Rothenberger, Brooklyn, New York

17. **Pushing** The same obstacle is used for pushing as for pulling. Pushing appears to be more challenging to the very young.

Elements are: Moves obstacle the full distance; places hands in "push" position (grasps or places hands against sides of bench at end); exerts force in line with resistance; keeps contact with object; applies force steadily after start; controls direction; uses long open stance at start; adjusts body appropriately to task and method (lowers body when pushing with arms, contacts bench with body when "walking" the object forward, etc.).

Achievement is indicated by *success* (moving obstacle the full distance), usually reached at age 2, and use of the elements. *Basic pattern* is attained by success and body adjustment appropriate to the method and is usual at age 2½.

18. **Running** This is one of the most demanding activities and therefore essentially developmental. Running requires much of the heart, lungs, and muscles. For the young child it also makes demands on the nervous system for all parts of the body must be moved in harmony; the arms and legs must be used alternately, symmetrically, and yet with synchronous timing; contraction and relaxation must alternate smoothly; an even rhythm must be maintained; balance makes new demands as strides lengthen and ground is covered rapidly.

Elements are: Covers the full distance (30-50 feet); inclines body forward at start; symmetry in leg action; symmetry in arm action; uses limbs in opposition; elbows well bent; lifts knees well in front; controls direction; toes point ahead; uses ball-of-foot contact.

Achievement consists of *success* (runs the designated distance), commonly attained at age 2, and use of the elements listed. It is also indicated by the speed with which the child runs. *Basic pattern* is established when opposition is used consistently (by most children at age 4).

19. *Running high jump*   This task requires an adjustable bar and a soft landing area; of the child it demands propulsion, balance, and confidence. Practice should be given at levels where the child is confident and can achieve success before trying for greater heights.

Elements are: Clearing the bar with a leap (from one foot to the other) or jump (from both feet to both or the same foot), checks run on approaching bar; takes off from one foot; lowers center of gravity over bar (by assuming a lying or lowered position of body); uses arms for elevation; accelerates opposite arm with trailing foot; lands on one foot; controls landing.

Achievement consists of *success* (clearing the bar at any height—but not by stepping over!), which is common at age 4½, and demonstration of the elements listed. Achievement is also indicated by the height of the jump. *Basic pattern* is attained when takeoff is preceded by a leading elevation of both arms and this also is attained at age 4½. In athletic competition the high jump has become highly stylized and the most successful methods vary widely from the basic pattern and from each other; nevertheless, many of the elements listed remain in the movement patterns used successfully in athletic competition.

20. *Skipping*   This is the second of the two-part rhythmic locomotor tasks. Children skip almost as spontaneously as they run but it is a later development and is probably elicited in part by imitation and certainly also by rhythmic stimulation.

Elements are: Maintains a skip over the prescribed distance (20-30 feet); alternates feet evenly; uses arms for balance; uses limbs in opposition; uses ball of foot contact; moves in direct path; uneven rhythm (short-long) but steady; skip is symmetrical (alike on both sides).

Achievement may be measured by *success* (at least four successive skips), usually attained at age 4½, and by use of the elements listed. *Basic pattern* is achieved when the child covers a distance of twenty feet with a steady, rhythmic skip; this is usual at age 6.

21. *Sliding*   The third of the two-part rhythmic locomotor tasks is sliding. Movement is sideward (right or left) and in an uneven

This child is using ball-of-foot action, uncommon at this age (4½). The skip is light and easy but arms are used together rather than in opposition.

rhythm with the foot on that side leading and the other foot following; the body faces forward so that progression is at right angles to body facing. This movement is much like galloping (also two-part) but the facing and sideward progression are difficult for very young children.

Elements are: Maintains body facing forward; leads with preferred foot; uses arms for balance; controls direction; uneven rhythm but steady; can lead with "other" foot; can change direction (and lead) smoothly.

Achievement is indicated by *success* (four or more successive slides in same direction), commonly reached by age 4, and demonstration of the elements given. At 4½ most children can slide in either direction. *Basic pattern* is demonstrated by sliding over the prescribed distance with steadiness and consistent rhythm and is usually demonstrated at age 5½.

22. *Standing broad jump* In this task the takeoff is from a mark on a flat surface and from both feet, the objective being to cover distance. A soft landing is essential; balance in landing should be maintained forward as stepping or falling backward reduces the distance covered.

26 Movement of the Young Child: Ages Two to Six

Children under three may not be able to perform this task except from an elevated takeoff; a box or small platform 12-18 inches high is suggested.

Elements are: Covers space forward; takes off from mark (no elevation); uses arms in preparation; uses arms forward-upward, leading the jump; uses two-foot takeoff; bends knees well in preparation; controls landing forward; accelerates with leg movement in air.

The arms are still used in winglike fashion in this jump from an elevation, at age 3. Note also that the left foot precedes the right in the preparation for a heel-first landing.
Photograph by Don Holt, Davis, California

Achievement is indicated by *success* (uses a true jump with two-foot takeoff to cover space) and the inclusion of the elements listed; success is usual at age 2½. The distance of the jump is also a criterion of achievement. *Basic pattern* is achieved with success when the arms lead the jump in paired movement; i.e., they are used symmetrically slightly ahead of the takeoff and in the direction of flight (forward-upward). Basic pattern is common from age 2½.

23. ***Throwing a small ball*** A used tennis ball is satisfactory here since it is small and soft. Throws should be varied to achieve specific targets and purposes. For this task, the writer encouraged the children to

throw as far as possible hoping to elicit a vigorous movement involving all parts of the body (total body assembly).

Elements are: Forward projection of the ball; sideward stance (feet placed at right angles to the line of flight; shifts weight in preparation;° uses body rotation;° throws with right hand (or left); uses overarm throw; is consistent in style of throw; follows through;° cocks (hyperextends and abducts) and uses wrist.

Achievement consists of *success* (projects ball forward), usually attained at age 2, and use of the elements listed; this may also be assessed by distance of the throw. *Basic pattern* is attained with success and the use of two or more of the starred (°) elements indicating some degree of total body assembly; this is usual from age 4.

This four year old has exaggerated his leg lift but is assuming the sideward stance and weight transfer necessary in preparation for distance throwing.
Photograph by Philipp Rothenberger, Brooklyn, New York

24. **Walking** At age 2 the child walks with confidence but he is still a novice; the older child (at 4 or 5) may display self-consciousness when walking for an observer unless he is given some related task which challenges him; the child should be observed from the side and also as he walks directly to the observer.

Elements are: Covers the prescribed distance (20-30 feet); alternates legs symmetrically; uses arms for balance; uses limbs in opposition; toes ahead; walks in straight line; heel strikes ground first; body is well aligned (erect, balanced).

Achievement consists of *success* (covers the distance with a walk), attained at age 2 or earlier, and use of the elements listed. *Basic pattern* is achieved when walking with symmetrical use of the arms and legs and no marked deviation in body alignment; basic pattern is usual at age 3.

At two the heel-toe sequence of foot placement may show up clearly in walking as it does here.
Photograph by Michael D. Sullivan, Washington, D.C.

25. *Walking the beam* The beam consists of a 2-by-4-inch board 8 feet long slightly elevated from the floor (see Appendix p. 108). For the task the 4-inch side is used until the age of 5 when the 2-inch side is employed. A great many balance activities may be practiced on this beam and it is useful for both indoor and outdoor play.

Elements are: Walks the full length (8 feet); keeps feet on the beam; uses arms for balance; toes ahead; moves forward continuously; moves forward at a steady pace; uses arms in opposition.

Achievement consists of *success* (walks the full length of the beam with not more than one step off), commonly attained at age 3, and use of the elements, also in progressing to the 2-inch width.

Movement Tasks   29

Basic pattern consists of success (on the 4-inch beam until 5 years of age) with toes ahead and arms contributing to balance; this is usual at age 4 on the 4-inch beam but is not usually attained on the 2-inch beam at either 5 or 6.

The five year old can walk a two-inch beam and the rungs of a ladder but it is a challenging task.

SUMMARY

Table 1 summarizes the contents of this chapter listing the activities and showing the ages at which success and basic pattern may be expected. In using this information full allowance should be made for time differences in the maturation of normal children.

TABLE ONE
Ages of Success and Basic Pattern for Motor Tasks

Task	Age 2	Age 3	Age 4	Age 5	Age 6
Ascending stairs	S	S BP	S BP	S BP	S BP
Bouncing on board	ˢ	S	S BP	S	S
Bouncing large ball			ˢ ᴮᴾ	S ᴮᴾ	S
Carrying	S BP	S BP	S BP	S BP	S BP

Legend: S = success BP = basic pattern. Elevation of the symbol indicates the age plus six months, for example, *success* in bouncing on a board at 2½.

30 Movement of the Young Child: Ages Two to Six

Task	Age 2	Age 3	Age 4	Age 5	Age 6
Catching	<u>S</u>	S	S		S
Climbing	<u>S</u>	S	S BP	S BP	S BP
Creeping	S <u>BP</u>	S BP	S BP	S BP	S BP
Descending stairs	<u>S</u>	S	S BP	S BP	S BP
Figure-8-run				<u>S</u>	S
Forward roll	<u>S</u>	S	S	S BP	S
Galloping	S	S	S BP	S BP	S BP
Hanging		S	S BP	S BP	S BP
Hitting	<u>S</u>	S	S	S	S
Hopping			S <u>BP</u>	S BP	S BP
Kicking	S	S	S	S BP	S
Pulling	S	S	S BP	S BP	S BP
Pushing	S	S <u>BP</u>	S BP	S BP	S BP
Running	S	S	S BP	S BP	S BP
Running high jump		<u>S</u>	S <u>BP</u>	S BP	S BP
Skipping			<u>S</u>	S	S BP
Sliding			S	S <u>BP</u>	S BP
Standing broad jump	<u>S</u>	S <u>BP</u>	S BP	S BP	S BP
Throwing	S	S	S	S BP	S BP
Walking	S	S BP	S BP	S BP	S BP
Walking the beam		S	S BP	<u>S</u>	S

LEGEND: S = success BP = basic pattern. Elevation of the symbol indicates the age plus six months, for example, *success* in bouncing on a board at two-and-one-half.

References

Espenschade, Anna S. and Helen M. Eckert. "Motor Behavior in Early Childhood." *Motor Development*. Columbus, Ohio: Charles E. Merrill Publishing Co., 1967, Chap. 7.

Rarick, G. Lawrence. *Motor Development During Infancy and Childhood*. Madison, Wisconsin: College Printing and Typing Co., 1961.

Sinclair, Caroline B. *Movement and Movement Patterns of Early Childhood*. Richmond, Va.: State Department of Education, 1971. The full research report of the same title is filed with the Division of Educational Research and Statistics, State Department of Education; Richmond, Public Schools, Richmond, Va.; and Madison Memorial Library, Madison College, Harrisonburg, Va.

Films

How Children Move and *First We Must See*, extracted from the research filming, are available from the author (C. Sinclair, Naxera, Va. 23122). Rental fee per film $12.00.

chapter three

THE DEVELOPMENT OF PATTERN IN MOVEMENT

A common premise has been that learning is of conscious direction while maturation is dictated by the genes. However this is not so since the two cannot really be separated and one influences the other.

Many lower forms of life are born, live, move, feed, reproduce, and die by the dictates of a genetic system which predetermines these processes in large part, but these functions are still subject to the availability of food and the vicissitudes of weather and climate, premature death or crippling, mating conditions, etc.

Man's life span may be roughly divided into three periods almost equal in length. The first period is one of growth and development including infancy, childhood, and adolescence when the body proceeds toward full maturity and the learning process is rapidly accelerated. The second period is one of ripening and easy repair and replacement when the full physical potential is realized, healing is still readily achieved, and learning becomes more meaningful as well as more selective. The third is when deterioration exceeds growth and repair and physical aging begins though the learning process may still function well through most of the aging years if continuously exercised.

GENETIC INFLUENCES

In the first five years of the period of growth and development the genetic controls of the individual's movement are most apparent for it is during this time that the child gradually develops ways of moving which identify him as "man" and also characterize him as a particular person. Elizabeth B. Gardner, the physiologist, has written, "Man is born with already built-in nerve circuits designed to produce specific, coordinating patterns of alternating or synchronous muscle response."[1] It is these complexes of movement, goal oriented as to purpose but involuntary as to neural control, that are here designated as *movement patterns*. And to quote Gardner again, "Man's basic motor patterns are probably genetically coded and laid down during development as specifically structured, interconnected circuits."[2] She goes on to cite the significance of activity within the nerve nets, changing conditions of the environment, and proprioceptive feedback. The phenomenon of movement patterns keyed in developmental sequence to the maturation of the infant and young child has been explored by many investigators and clearly demonstrated by Myrtle B. McGraw,[3] N.C. Kephart,[4] Ruth B. Glassow,[5] Lolas E. Halverson,[6] Caroline B. Sinclair,[7] and others.

ENVIRONMENTAL INFLUENCES

The first essential for movement development in young children is good health including an intact nervous system; the second is space—with adequate control of hazards. Add as a third essential one or more

---

[1] Elizabeth B. Gardner, "Proprioceptive Reflexes", *Quest*, Monograph XII (May 1969), p. 1.
[2] Ibid., p. 2.
[3] Myrtle B. McGraw, *The Neuromuscular Maturation of the Human Infant*, reprint edition 1963-1966 (New York: Hafner Publishing Co., 1966), pp. 1-140.
[4] Jack D. Dunsing and Newell C. Kephart, "Motor Generalizations in Space and Time," *Learning Disorders*, Vol. 1, edited by Jerome Helmuth, (Seattle, Wash.: Special Child Publications of the Seattle Sequin Schools, 1965), pp. 77-121.
[5] John M. Cooper and Ruth B. Glassow, *Kinesiology* (St. Louis: The C.V. Mosby Co., 1963), pp. 193-98.
[6] Lolas Halverson, "Research in Motor Development—Implications for Program in Early Childhood Education," (Address to the Midwest Association for Health, Physical Education, and Recreation, Chicago, March 12, 1970).
[7] Caroline B. Sinclair, *Movement and Movement Patterns* (Richmond, Va.: Division of Educational Research and Statistics, State Department of Education, 1971), pp. 1-24.

parental figures who encourage and motivate, and good progress is predicted.

The child will move easily from oral and tactile exploration of objects to exploration by moving through and around his space—whatever it is; he will crawl, creep, walk, and run in due time. If furnishings permit he will climb up and down, go over and under, open and close doors, push and pull objects—and all in his own way—which is amazingly like that of millions of other children.

But, if his space is restricted, his clothes are too tight, or if he is not allowed on the floor, or on the ladder, or up a tree, his inborn motor complexes will *not* develop into smoothly operating movement patterns. The clumsy child may be a sufferer of slight brain damage but he may also be the product of a restrictive environment in the significant years of early childhood.

THE CHILD'S RESPONSE AND INTERACTION

Man is a product of his own activity. Nature endows each infant with potentials; it is his own activity that develops these. His life-sustaining activities function from birth but are strengthened and retained by use; this is true of circulation, digestion, respiration and other functions which in turn are stimulated and controlled by muscles and nerves through movement. The movements of work and play which allow man to move through life with efficiency and enjoyment are based upon common movement patterns such as walking, jumping, climbing, and throwing from which all of the highly specialized sport, dance, and work skills are developed. In early childhood this development proceeds when the child is provided with opportunities for eliciting the inborn movement patterns. The movement provides feedback both through the sensory organs and through social reaction (approval) which send him on to further practice and more refined and/or complex achievements. Thus interaction is of two kinds: 1) that which is provided by the nervous system and primarily through the proprioceptors and sensory nerve fibers which record position, direction, tension, and force and define success in sensory terms, and 2) that provided by *people* including self-realization of a goal. Both are significant for experiencing success; the small child seeks verification of achievement when he cries, "Look at me!" or runs to tell his mother that he "did it." It is interaction—of both kinds—which provides the input from which learning proceeds, spiraling ever upward to greater and higher levels.

THEORY OF PATTERNING

Current theory of movement patterning is based on these premises:

1. There are genetic syndromes of nerve-muscle relationships which can be excited at a subconscious level and which result in coordinated responses of two or more body parts.
2. The method of elicitation is in itself complex and developmental over a period of time.
3. Both input and output are involved in elicitation and development; that is, sensory stimulation is essential in preparing for, producing, and perfecting a given pattern and also in monitoring the performance of the pattern (output) toward further use.

A movement pattern does not just appear, fully ripened. Some appear in infancy, some at age two or three, some later. A few appear "in toto" or nearly so, others develop over a period of several months or even years. The neuromuscular complex is there and the nerve-net may be built-in, but upon how and when the child is motivated to use it will depend the appearance of pattern and his later achievement. Success has been claimed for the following methods: passive patterning (by one or more persons or by a machine) of the brain-damaged; self-patterning through creeping by the less injured; and cross-lateral emphasis for the underachiever. Although there is clinical evidence to support these claims, research findings have been unreliable, contradictory, or fragmentary.

Research (Halverson,[8] Sinclair,[9] Glassow[10]) does support the premise that the basic movement patterns can be established by children in early childhood.

STIMULATION AND FEEDBACK

To move is the delight of a small child and the movement itself may well be the goal—as the joy in his face will testify. But, nevertheless, his movement is goal oriented and he "thinks" the goal, not the process. The stimulation and the response should be simple. The needed movement pattern will emerge and more smoothly when the task is

---

[8]Lolas E. Halverson and Mary Ann Robertson, "A Study of Motor Pattern Development in Young Children," (Report at National Convention of American Association for Health, Physical Education, and Recreation Madison, University of Wisconsin, 1966).

[9]Sinclair, *Movement and Movement Patterns,* pp. 1-24.

[10]Cooper and Glassow, *Kinesiology,* pp. 193-98.

presented simply and the goal is meaningful to the child. To climb up the ladder is easily understood; to skip may mean little to the child but he can be motivated by demonstration or by listening to skipping music. A tangible goal ("run to the red mark") is helpful. Demonstration should be used not to set the pattern but to aid in its discovery.

Feedback is resident in the child's sensory experience and is reenforced by immediate repetition and by frequent practice; it is also enhanced by the child's expressed recognition of success and by the approval and encouragement of others. It follows that a good performance might well be repeated while to try again and again when experiencing errors and failure only reenforces the faulty pattern and produces frustration.

PATTERNS OF RELATED MOVEMENTS

Creeping and climbing Four-part movements are those in which the four limbs participate. Creeping is the action in which the baby first synchronizes movement in a four-part cross-lateral pattern. This requires a highly organized neuromuscular action for synchronous movement of opposite arm and leg. Both excitation and inhibition are involved as one leg is stopped as the other starts to move. It is on this complex demand that creeping has been judged an especially significant activity in the neurological development of the child. Climbing also involves both support by and movement of the four limbs. Young children climb readily and like to climb; they use both arms and legs but seldom develop the smooth synchronous, cross-lateral pattern usually demonstrated in creeping.

Known as opposition this alternating, synchronous action is a prominent element in many fundamental and derived movement patterns. It is one of the characteristics of efficient motor performance (see chapter four).

Walking and running The alternating pattern of opposite arm and leg is also evident in running and, to a lesser extent, in brisk walking. Walking and running are the most common forms of man's locomotion. The patterns of movement are similar, though in the young child the walk is keyed to balance while the run is adapted for greater speed—sometimes at the expense of balance! The adaptations for the run are progressive: the stance is narrowed, the stride is lengthened, the knee is lifted, the foot contact is shortened and reduced to ball-of-foot, the arm swing is reduced in arc and angle, and body lean is increased for a faster start. These changes, many of which were impossible when balance was a greater problem, accelerate the speed factor as the child increases in strength, size, and control.

Swimming and skating Swimming and skating include oppositional movement and are based on creeping (four-part) or walking (two-part) patterns.

In swimming a number of diversified propulsive patterns or strokes have been developed. Of these patterns the crawl, which closely resembles creeping, is most readily achieved by children who easily acquire a simplified "on demand" method of breathing; a modification is the "human stroke" or dog paddle with head out of water.

Two-part rhythms The gallop, slide, and skip are derived from the walk and are often called two-part rhythms or dance steps. Each step is preceded or followed by a shorter action which gives the step-pattern its characteristic uneven (*short-long* or *long-short*) two-beat rhythm.

The gallop is done with one foot leading (left or right), the body facing forward. The *step* is taken each time with the leading foot while the subsequent shorter action provides the follow step. Arms tend to move together rather than in opposition.

In the slide, usually performed facing at right angles to direction, the leading foot (left or right) steps to the side and the other follows with a quick closing step to provide the uneven rhythm. Arms are usually held sideward near shoulder height and move only a little.

The skip requires an alternating lead of the feet as in the walk and each step is initiated with a slight hop on the supporting foot. Arms are used in opposition although the small child may stabilize them for better balance.

In all of these forms the step is on the long and accented beat (music or other accompaniment) and the hop or follow-step is the interim (between beats) action; thus the gallop, slide, and skip share a rhythmic pattern but vary in step-pattern; each has a distinctive appearance and "feeling."

Moving through space One of the identifying characteristics of jumping is unsupported movement through space. In this sense a hop, a leap, a spring from a diving board or other surface, and some falls are similar. Jumping is a form of locomotion but it has the special quality of exerting force explosively or requiring the assembly of body parts for *power*. Jumping is an action in which one or both feet exert a propulsive force against resistance to project the body upward and sometimes outward; the flight and the landing, which must of course occur eventually, are controlled in various ways. The takeoff may occur from one or both feet and may be augmented by a variety of surfaces and devices.

An identifying characteristic of all these self-propulsive acts is the preparatory flexing of the joints of the supporting leg (or legs) and the strong extensor thrust of these joints against the supporting surface at takeoff. This propulsion is assisted and preceded by the lift of the arms in the direction of the movement and by the auxiliary movements of head, body, arms, and legs adapted to the particular purpose of the flight.

Similarly the landing, for safety and control, is characterized (except in diving) by a quickly controlled flexion of those body parts making first contact, the use of the arms for balance, and the conversion of momentum into further movements in the line of direction. For example, the jumper, tumbler, or clown may land on one or both feet and run a few steps or he may pull himself into a close tuck and do a forward roll.

Striking and throwing Balls are the most universal play and sports implements. They are of many sizes and weights and vary to some degree in shape and surface. Many games involve throwing, striking, and kicking (which is a form of striking the ball). These actions have much in common though striking most often involves elongating the arm with a bat or paddle. The ball is usually thrown with one hand or kicked with one foot, and the striking instrument (for convenience called the *striker*) is commonly held in one hand (tennis, badminton) or with both hands on one side (baseball). These actions are usually unilateral movements.

In throwing and striking, the stance for greatest distance is sideward with the left foot forward (for right-handed performers) and the body facing at right angles to the line of direction. Preparation is with axial movement of the body to the right, transfer of weight to the right foot, and backward movement (to the right) of the arm, hand, and object. Speed requires movement through maximum space in the shortest possible time, hence forward movement is at high speed and in sequence from feet through the body to forearm and wrist. The final action is for balance and control *after* the ball is on its way. Usually called the follow-through this action consists of continuing the propelling action which is checked by a step or two in the line of direction and converted into readiness for the next play.

The participation of all body parts in the action from rear foot to propelling wrist and hand is known as *total body assembly* and the speed at which it occurs will largely determine the distance of the throw or the hit.

In kicking the action pattern will differ in allowing the foot to move from backward to forward. The body will face forward. If the child approaches in a run the preparation will be a part of the running action. If the kick is low and level the opposite arm will move forward with the kicking foot; if the kick is high both arms will move up and then sideward to assist in balance following the kick.

The basic patterns of throwing and kicking are complex and not often achieved before age five; the hitting pattern is further complicated by the need for accuracy in meeting the ball and is seldom achieved before school age. Immature patterns in these tasks persist at all ages especially among girls and women.

Pushing, pulling, and carrying These tasks require a mobilization of the body parts in a team effort to exert greater muscular force than any one part of the body is capable of producing. To push or pull a heavy object the muscles of arms, legs, and trunk must work together in *total body assembly* to move the object and to keep it moving. To lift a heavy object, to carry it, and to put it down in a controlled manner also requires sustained and forceful effort. Even two year olds will exhibit great effort and will persist in these tasks; they will experiment with different methods and achieve success in different ways. Almost from the beginning, young children will bend the knees and use the leg extensors in lifting a weight; they will lower the trunk in order to bring the force more nearly in line with the resistance when pushing and pulling; and they will grasp the object in a good pulling or pushing position. These elements of the patterns change little through early childhood but greater achievement comes with increased strength and size and with more experience and practice.

LIKENESS IN MOVEMENT PATTERNS

Like elements can be identified in many fundamental movements; some such as balance, rhythm, and opposition are characteristic of nearly all movement.

The body is assembled (all parts work together) to apply force simultaneously—rapidly and briefly when power is needed for one mighty effort; slowly and with sustained effort when strength is needed as for moving a heavy object; and by rapid sequential movement of body parts over a wide range to develop speed as in throwing or hitting a ball. Young children demonstrate integrated movement long before they are able to achieve such complex action step by step in a planned movement. Again, this integrated use of the body parts is called *total body assembly* (TBA). This characteristic and several others will be discussed in chapter four.

ACHIEVING BASIC PATTERNS

Observation indicates that basic movement patterns are achieved in different ways. Many patterns such as walking are acquired over a period of time and by repeated and persistent efforts; some are developed from a more elementary form—running is preceded by walking and is developed over several years; some, like hopping, appear rather suddenly—yesterday the child could not hop, today he can—and the pattern changes little except to become more rhythmic and graceful.

There are several guides that may be useful in helping the child to achieve the basic movement patterns:

1. Give the child an opportunity to perform the motor task when he is able to achieve a degree of success. See chapter two for probable age. If he is unsuccessful let him try again but do not press him.
2. Set a goal for the task which the child will understand and enjoy and stress the *what* rather than the *how*. For example, ask him to jump over the bar but do not tell him how to do it; in achieving the goal he will call upon his own resources and find his own way—the pattern will emerge or develop if the child is ready.
3. If possible see that the experience is pleasant and gratifying. Safety is essential and comfort is certainly desirable. Prevent accidents and discomfort by using good equipment and soft landing surfaces and by lending a helping hand when needed.
4. If a child's performance is faulty he may try again for better result but do not allow him to practice a faulty action repeatedly for this may delay or prevent the emergence of the appropriate pattern. It is better to wait a few days or weeks.
5. A child will usually indicate his unreadiness for a task, and such indication should be honored. Sometimes he needs only a little waiting; sometimes he will learn from watching other children working at the same task.
6. Parents and teachers should restrain themselves from being overprotective and overhelpful. A certain degree of independence is necessary for self-discovery.
7. Basic movement patterns do not usually require direct instruction. They will emerge at the appropriate time. The teacher's

task is to provide the challenge, the opportunity, and the encouragement for eliciting them.
8. When the child first discovers a new way of moving it may appear clumsy and awkward but he will usually delight in its performance. The teacher must accept his achievement and share his enjoyment.
9. The child first experiences success in reaching the goal of a new motor task; in time a basic movement pattern emerges; still later, and by means of practice and with skillful teaching, the child will achieve an efficient and graceful use of the pattern in a myriad of variations and combinations.

References

Godfrey, Barbara B., and Newell C. Kephart. *Movement Patterns and Motor Education*. New York: Appleton-Century-Crofts, 1969.

Halverson, Lolas E. "Development of Motor Patterns in Young Children," *Quest*. Monograph 6 (May 1966), 51-52.

Kephart, Newell C. *The Slow Learner in the Classroom*. 2nd ed. Columbus, Ohio: Charles E. Merrill Publishing Co., 1971.

McGraw, Myrtle B. *The Neuromuscular Maturation of the Human Infant*. Reprint. New York: Hafner Publishing Co., 1963.

Sinclair, Caroline B. *Movement and Movement Patterns of Early Childhood*. Richmond, Va.: State Department of Education, 1971.

Wickstrom, Ralph L. *Fundamental Motor Patterns*. Philadelphia: Lea and Febiger, 1970.

chapter four

GENERAL CHARACTERISTICS OF MOVEMENT

The patterns of fundamental movements have much in common. The previous chapter groups together some of those which are most alike and explores their commonality. It is the purpose of this chapter to present eight general characteristics of movement which have been identified by the author and given special study. It is thought that the successful attainment and use of one or more of these characteristics at an appropriate age might be valuable in the appraisal of motor development. Conversely, the study of these characteristics may lead to better curriculum in physical education for preschool and elementary school children.

Characteristics common to many improvement tasks which were selected for special study include:

1. Opposition (the synchronized use of opposite hand and foot in the upright position and cross-laterality in quadripedal movement) and symmetry (including foot-over-foot action in climbing and descending).
2. Dynamic balance (the ability to maintain equilibrium while moving).
3. Total body assembly (using the parts of the body as levers to acquire speed or force against resistance or for power release in a combination of speed and force).

4. Rhythmic two-part locomotion (as in the gallop, the slide, and the skip).
5. Eye-hand efficiency in manual response to a static or moving object.
6. Agility (maneuverability of the body).
7. Postural adjustment.
8. Dominance (side preference for paired parts).

An indefinite number of characteristics may be observed as common to many motor tasks. Those selected were chosen because they are readily recognized if present and because they seem to promise well as criteria in the child's progressive development. Charles McCloy[1] lists thirty-seven factors, some having a number of subfactors, for motor activities. He also lists other factors concerned with physical growth, character, personality, and cardiovascular condition and, thus, related also to motor ability.

Motor learning is indeed complex and movement development is dependent upon many factors. The exploration of these eight characteristics is intended to aid in the critical observation of young children and to give some simple clues for the appraisal of their movement.

SYMMETRY AND OPPOSITION OF THE LIMBS

The characteristic of symmetry is displayed in many actions where the movement is bilateral (as in the forward roll) or where the limbs move alternately and in an oppositional pattern (right hand and left foot, then left hand and right foot) as in walking or running. Table 2 shows the percentage of subjects demonstrating symmetry and opposition at ages two to six.

Whether or not a child demonstrates this characteristic is especially indicative of his movement development as follows:

At two for opposition in running
At three for ascending stairs foot-over-foot
At four for opposition in running, kicking, and climbing
At five for descending stairs foot-over-foot

The human being is a bilateral animal with two almost identical arms and legs and with the right side of the body very similar to the left. The body is thus built for symmetrical movement and this symmetry

---

[1]Charles Harold McCloy and Norma Dorothy Young, *Tests and Measurements in Health and Physical Education*, 3rd ed. (New York: Appleton-Century-Crofts, Inc. 1954), pp. 3-13.

TABLE TWO
Percentage of Subjects Demonstrating Symmetry and Opposition

	With Synchrony in Creeping	With Synchrony in Climbing	Of Feet in Ascending Stairs	Of Feet in Descending Stairs	Of Feet in Climbing (Ladder)	Of Hand and Foot in Walk	Of Hand and Foot in Run	Of Hand and Foot in Kick	Of Hand and Foot in Skip
	%	%	%	%	%	%	%	%	%
Age 2	23	03	14	03	17	46	80	50	00
Age 3	55	30	89	12	55	59	79	48	04
Age 4	45	29	100	84	65	59	74	50	12
Age 5	44	Jungle	—	92	Jungle	67	91	72	16
Age 6	56	Gym°	—	94	Gym°	67	100	55	44

°Pattern varies, not regular as on ladder.

43

which is sometimes synchronous and sometimes alternating is desirable for many actions. If the action is one-sided (as in throwing) adjustments must be made. Adjustments are also made for other purposes—to achieve balance, to carry an object, to protect an injury. Asymmetry which is consistent and which persists beyond an obvious need for it should always be investigated; it may be indicative of soreness, deformity, weakness, fear, or there may be some other cause.

DYNAMIC BALANCE

Dynamic balance is the characteristic which, in other studies, has been most often found to have a positive correlation with reading readiness and other estimates of school achievement. Table 3 shows the percentage of subjects demonstrating dynamic balance at ages two to six.

TABLE THREE
Percentage of Subjects Demonstrating Dynamic Balance

	In Bounce on Board	On Walking Beam	In Hop	Both Feet
	%	%	%	%
Age 2	60	43	00	00
Age 3	70	65	28	00
Age 4	83	100	71	13
Age 5	-	2-inch 56	96	96
Age 6	-	2-inch 77	100	100

This investigator found indications of significance of dynamic balance in the child's movement development especially as follows:

At two in walking the four-inch beam
At three in hopping
At four in hopping (but less significant than at three)
At five in walking the two-inch beam
At six in walking the two-inch beam (but less significant than at five)

Dynamic balance seems to increase steadily from ages two to six and thereafter. H.G. Seashore suggests that it is fully attained at about eleven years.[2] It is a great asset in dance, sports, and physical work and appears to have special significance for the young child as he deals with the erect position, learns to control his body in space, and relates himself to the world about him.

TOTAL BODY ASSEMBLY

Total body assembly (TBA) is exhibited in a variety of ways and in the performance of most motor tasks. The author has studied it in three categories as previously described (see p. 38): TBA for strength (force), TBA for speed, TBA for power. The percentage of subjects demonstrating total body assembly at ages two to six is given in table 4.

Total body assembly was identified and deemed especially indicative of the child's movement development as follows:

TBA for strength

    At age two in pulling and carrying
    At age three in pulling
    At age four in carrying

Criterion: Subjects were able to perform the task successfully.

TBA for speed

    At age two in hitting
    At age three in hitting and throwing
    At age four in hitting and throwing
    At age six in hitting

Criterion: (In this analysis accuracy in hitting the ball was disregarded.) Subjects demonstrated three of the four elements starred on pages 20 and 21.

TBA for power

    At age two in the standing broad jump (from elevation)
    At age three in the running high jump
    At age four in the standing broad jump
    At age five in the running high jump

Criterion: Subjects demonstrated appropriate lead of arms timed with the jump.

Total body assembly is the most complex characteristic studied; it is not easy for the inexperienced observer to identify. For self-training

---

[2]H.G. Seashore, "The Development of a Beam Walking Test and Its Use in Measuring Development of Balance in Children," *Research Quarterly*, 18 (1947): 258.

the observer should watch many trials of a movement and look for one element at a time until several can be identified at once. Practice with film and a hand-turned projector is invaluable.

TABLE FOUR
Percentage of Subjects Demonstrating Total Body Assembly

	Speed		Power		Force		
	In Hitting	In Throwing	In Standing Broad Jump	In Running High Jump	In Pulling	In Pushing	In Carrying
	%	%	%	%	%	%	%
Age 2	23	33	28	07	50	63	36
Age 3	52	24	50	45	72	83	48
Age 4	35	48	64	80	90	71	84
Age 5	60	68	76	88	92	76	64
Age 6	72	88	83	94	100	100	61

RHYTHMIC TWO-PART LOCOMOTION

Because rhythm is such an important characteristic in movement and because the gallop, slide, and skip have a definite and identical rhythmic pattern and yet are recognized as separate ways of moving, these three motor tasks were chosen as a unit for study. They are of special interest since all are accomplished by most children between the ages of two and five and usually in a sequence which suggests that one is preparation for another. The percentage of subjects demonstrating rhythmic two-part locomotion at ages two to six is given in table 5.

Abilities in galloping, sliding, and skipping may be especially useful criteria in determining the child's development in movement as follows:

At age two success in galloping (one-foot lead)
At age four success in galloping and sliding (both leads)
At age five success in skipping

TABLE FIVE
Percentage of Subjects Demonstrating Two-Part Rhythmic Locomotion

	In Galloping	In Galloping Both Ways	In Sliding	In Sliding Both Ways	In Skipping
	%	%	%	%	%
Age 2	50	00	00	00	00
Age 3	76	14	34	24	7
Age 4	92	58	77	13	52
Age 5	88	68	100	88	89
Age 6	89	83	100	94	100

EYE-HAND EFFICIENCY

The author has chosen this term instead of the more common term "eye-hand coordination" believing it to be more descriptive of the attribute under study. Eye-hand efficiency can be studied in many situations. The two situations chosen are in catching and hitting a ball: in catching the response was to a moving ball; in hitting the response was with a moving object to a stationary ball. Table 6 shows the percentage of subjects demonstrating eye-hand efficiency. Note the sharp drop when a small ball was used for catching at age five.

TABLE SIX
Percentage of Subjects Demonstrating Eye-Hand Efficiency

	In Catching a Ball	In Hitting a Ball	In Bouncing a Ball
	%	%	%
Age 2	67	46	-
Age 3	79	48	63°
Age 4	94	58	100°
Age 5	60	52	100°
Age 6	72	78	89

°Age is year given plus six months.

Eye-hand efficiency thus demonstrated was found to be especially indicative of significance in movement development:

At age three in catching
At age four in catching
At age five in catching and hitting

As pointed out in chapter two most children were unsuccessful in catching and hitting small balls at age five and many were not successful at six. Eye adjustment and team work of the eyes seem to be unequal to the tasks in these early years.

AGILITY

Agility embodies factors of speed, flexibility, and motor educability or "know how." It is a quality essential to many sports (football, basketball, and others) and can be acquired in childhood since it is not dependent on great strength or size. Table 7 shows the percentage of subjects demonstrating agility in two tasks. The agility demonstrated in the forward roll at age three is significantly related to movement development.

TABLE SEVEN
Percentage of Subjects Demonstrating Agility in Two Tasks

	In Forward Roll	In Figure-8-Run
	%	%
Age 2	23	-
Age 3	35	00°
Age 4	42	25°
Age 5	64	40°
Age 6	41	44°

°Age is year given plus six months.

POSTURAL ADJUSTMENT

This characteristic must vary with the task and is included in the elements listed for many of the motor tasks. The percentage of subjects demonstrating postural adjustment in three tasks is given in table 8.

Postural adjustment was given special study for significance in motor development and findings indicated that erect, balanced posture in walking is related to motor development at ages three and six but not at the other ages studied. The rationale for this is not clear. A child of three may or may not have attained the balance necessary for walking easily and erectly; at age four and later this may be no challenge for him unless there are structural difficulties or other problems. The author noted elsewhere that self-consciousness and restrictions were more noticeable among the six year olds than in the same children at an earlier age; thus postural adjustment may again be a more variable factor at six.

TABLE EIGHT
Percentage of Subjects Demonstrating Postural Adjustment in Three Tasks

| | *In Walking* | *In Running* | *In Standing Broad Jump* |
	%	%	%
Age 2	73	70	80
Age 3	62	72	76
Age 4	77	94	81
Age 5	84	100	96
Age 6	67	89	89

DOMINANCE

Dominance or side preference is a peculiarly human characteristic, most noticeable in the prevalence of right-handedness and most significant in the control and development of the left hemisphere of the brain as compared to that of the right. The logical picture of a right-handed person as also right-footed, right-eyed, right-eared, and left-hemispheric (the left side of the brain controls the right side of the body) can be varied by one or more left-sided preferences and by greater or lesser degrees of preference. Professional literature is rife with instances of the child who encounters difficulty in motor performance, social adjustment and/or school achievement, and who also exhibits mixed dominance. The research is inconclusive. Table 9 shows the distribution of hand and foot preference which was predominantly right at all ages.

When right dominance was singled out for special study it was found to have low correlation with motor score, with teachers' estimates of achievement, and with reading readiness. However, it was observed that certain children who were late in developing dominance were retarded in motor performance, social adjustment, or school achievement. See chapter six, "Case Studies."

The tendency to be right or left handed and otherwise right or left dominant is believed to be of genetic origin which varies in degree so that a person may be strong in preference, moderate in preference, or have little or no preference. In the latter case he may develop true ambidexterity which is rare but has certain obvious advantages. It has been suggested that parents and educators might devote more time to helping the child to use both sides of the body well. On the other hand the child who develops consistent dominance by four years of age seems to be more assured and finds the world less confusing than those children who do not establish dominance until later. Left-handed children are often delayed in establishing dominance.

Children can be helped if observers recognize and record preference for hand and foot; by screening tests for dominance of eye and ear; by encouraging the use of the *right* side of the body unless preference for the left is clearly indicated; by encouraging unilateral preference unless mixed dominance is clearly indicated; and by having dominance records ready for study in connection with any problem that may develop. The teacher or parent should be aware that the factor of dominance has been associated with some cases of underachievement and with dyslexia though it is probable that other factors are also involved.

MEASURING ACHIEVEMENT

Achievement in motor tasks is commonly measured in units of time or distance (How far can you throw? How high can you jump? How fast can you run fifty yards?) or in numbers of successful tries (How many baskets out of ten tries? What is his batting percentage?). A more important criterion for the young child than the results of the effort would seem to be the way in which he does it; this idea would seem to be in harmony with the child's goal which is often the effort or task involved rather than the end results.

TABLE NINE
Distribution of Hand and Foot Preference in Throwing and Kicking

	Total No. Subjects	Like Preference	Right Hand Right Foot	Left Hand Left Foot	Mixed Preference	Right Hand Left Foot	Left Hand Right Foot	Uncertain	Hand or Foot
Age 2	30*	24	24	0	4	3	1	2	H 2
Age 3	29	25	25	0	0	0	0	4	F 4
Age 4	31	24	24	0	1	0	1	6	H 3 F 3 B 2
Age 5	25	21	20	1	1	0	1	3	H 2 F 1
Age 6	18	16	15	1	2	1	1	0	0

*Add first figures in each of three sections for total.

51

It may be said with some assurance that the general characteristics of symmetry, dynamic balance, total body assembly, rhythm, eye-hand efficiency, agility, and postural adjustment have an important contribution to make to an individual's development and further that a child's motor development may be studied and appraised by noting these characteristics in appropriate motor tasks. As previously indicated, certain of these characteristics have been found significant at designated ages as indices of motor score. The author recommends their use in clinical appraisal rather than as tests of movement development. In such appraisal the child's age in years and months should be considered and he should be observed over a period of time; his steady improvement is a more important criterion than is the attainment of a standard for his age. In appraisal the observer should be guided by the child's use of several general characteristics appropriate to his age, rather than depending upon a single characteristic even though it may have high correlation with motor development.

References

Huelsman, Charles B., Jr. "Six Concepts of Vision." *School Health Review*. 1, no. 4 (November 1970): 29-31.

Hunt, Valerie E. "Movement Behavior: A Model for Action." *Quest*. Monograph II (April 1964).

Sinclair, Caroline B. *Movement and Movement Patterns in Early Childhood*. Richmond, Va.: State Department of Education, 1971.

chapter five

DIFFERENCES IN THE MOVEMENT OF CHILDREN

Movement is a developing process during the early years of childhood and adolescence. The period of early childhood is especially important to this development since it is during these years that the fundamental movements should be established and that the basic patterns for them so readily emerge.

The similarities of the movement of children in the preschool years are apparent when they are given similar opportunities; the differences which occur are clearly related to age and less closely related to sex, race, intelligence (quotient), and school achievement. It is obvious that other factors are also related.

Age

That children improve in their ability to move as they grow older is commonly recognized. Evidence is offered by increases in the speed, force, and power they are able to generate and by the developing complexity of their movement. More objective evidence is offered by increasing motor scores (table 10), by the development and maturation of movement patterns (chapter three), by better time and distance as measured in four athletic events (table 11), and by positive correlations of age and motor score at all ages (table 12). Since table

12 gives correlations within the age group (for example, of all four year olds together, ranked by age in months and days), it is clear that age differences of less than a year are important and especially so prior to age three. When children are classified in age groups teachers and par-

TABLE TEN
Means of Motor Scores by Age and Sex

	Age 2	Age 3	Age 4	Age 5	Age 6
Boys	28.1	39.3	53.3	56.0	64.0
Girls	32.3	41.2	50.0	50.6	57.7
Both	31.0	40.5	51.6	52.2	60.9

TABLE ELEVEN
Means of Measured Jumps (2), Runs, and Throws by Age and Sex

	Running high jump (inches)	Standing broad jump (inches)	50-ft. run (seconds)	Distance throw (feet)
Boys 3½	8.5	19.0°	5.74	
Girls 3½	12.0	25.8°	5.57	
Both 3½	10.6	20.9°	5.58	
Boys 4½	12.0	31.0	4.70	19.0°
Girls 4½	17.3	25.8	4.63	17.5°
Both 4½	16.0	30.4	4.65	18.5°
Boys 5½	17.3	39.6	4.53	44.6
Girls 5½	19.0	37.3	4.65	25.0
Both 5½	17.3	38.3	4.58	35.7
Boys 6	22.0	45.3	4.19	57.4
Girls 6	20.7	41.6	4.20	31.9
Both 6	21.3	42.1	4.19	44.6

° These distances were recorded at age given minus six months.

TABLE TWELVE
Correlation of General Factors with Motor Scores

	Age within Group	Sex: Male	Race: White	IQ	DQ	Achievement Teacher's Estimate	Reading Readiness Percentile Score	Level of .05 Significance for r
Age 2	.67	−.22	−.33	.25	.14	—		.349
Age 3	.60	−.14	−.22	.04	.38	.36		.355
Age 4	.12	.29	−.17	.05		.30		.347
Age 5	.25	.21	−.30	.03		.23		.381
Age 6	.12	.41	−.27	.15		.04	.17	.444

ents should be especially aware of age differences within the groups. A child who is six in October may have abilities more like those children in the five-year group than like those of the other and older sixes, and a late three year old may be far ahead of another child who is just past two. Conversely, a child of nearly six on October first may find the tasks offered the five year olds very easy and lacking in challenge. Rank by age within the age group appears as a very significant factor in placing a subject among the highest or lowest in motor achievement in his group.

And yet there is much variation among preschoolers of similar age in movement development. Wide ranges of motor scores mark the performances of all age groups and many individuals. Children who are in need of prolonged remedial programs are usually below age level in a large number of tasks or show a marked and consistent insufficiency in two or more tasks or characteristics. For most deviations a little help given at the right time can be expected to bring effective results.

Sex

Until the age of four boys and girls move very much alike and their achievement is similar, with girls having a slight advantage especially before three. At age four boys appear to forge ahead especially in those tasks requiring strength and in throwing (see tables 10, 11, and 13). All aspects of total body assembly are demonstrated more often at this age by boys than by girls. At three and after, boys are more proficient

TABLE THIRTEEN
Means of Task Scores by Age and Sex

	Age 2 Boys	Age 2 Girls	Age 3 Boys	Age 3 Girls	Age 4 Boys	Age 4 Girls	Age 5 Boys	Age 5 Girls	Age 6 Boys	Age 6 Girls
Ascending stairs	2.3	2.5	3.4	3.2	3.6°	3.5°	4.3°	4.0°	4.3	4.2
Bouncing a ball			1.0°	2.0°	2.0°	3.0°	3.7°	3.3°	4.1	3.1
Bouncing	1.3	1.1	1.9	2.1	2.6	2.4				
Carrying	2.4	3.7	3.1	3.4	3.5	3.7	3.8	3.5	4.2	3.3
Catching	.7	1.5	2.3	2.2	2.6	2.1	2.3	1.4	2.8	1.4
Climbing	1.7	1.9	2.5	2.6	3.9	2.6	3.1	2.9	4.3	3.6
Creeping	1.9	3.4	3.5	2.9	3.8	3.7	3.4	3.3	4.3	3.1
Descending stairs	1.6	1.8	2.1	2.2	3.0	2.9	3.0°	3.0°	4.0	3.9
Figure-8-run			.0°	.7°	2.0°	1.7°	2.3°	2.5°	3.6	2.2
Forward roll	2.1	1.5	1.5	2.5	2.4	2.3	3.0	3.2	2.8	2.4
Galloping	.5	1.3	2.0	1.7	2.8	3.7	3.1	3.5	3.4	4.0
Hanging	1.6	2.3	1.3	2.6	3.0	3.0	2.9	2.9	3.3	3.0
Hitting	1.6	.5	1.5	1.4	1.4	.8	2.9	.8	2.1	2.8
Hopping	0	0	.2	1.0	2.3	2.5	3.1	3.3	4.0	3.7

56

	2.2	2.3	2.7	2.6	2.9	2.7	3.2	3.1	3.2	2.3
Kicking										
Pulling	3.0	2.0	2.6	2.5	4.1	3.5	4.2	3.3	3.8	3.1
Pushing	1.9	2.4	3.1	3.2	4.3	2.1	4.6	3.5	3.7	3.2
Running	1.8	2.1	2.6	2.7	3.4	3.1	3.5	3.8	3.4	3.3
Running high jump	.3	.4	1.4	1.7	2.7	2.2	3.0	3.5	3.1	3.1
Skipping	0	0	0	.2	1.3	2.1	2.0	2.3	3.6	2.7
Sliding	0	0	.7	1.1	2.4	2.3	2.5	3.2	3.9	4.3
Standing broad jump	1.8	1.8	2.5	2.7	3.5	3.1	3.5	4.3	3.2	4.1
Throwing	2.0	2.1	3.7	2.1	3.8	2.3	3.8	2.3	3.6	3.0
Walking	2.6	3.0	3.3	3.1	3.1	3.1	3.6	3.0	3.7	3.7
Walking a beam	.1	.4	1.6	2.3	3.0	3.0	2.3	1.5	3.0	1.8

*These at age given plus six months.

than girls in many motor tasks and this difference is maintained with great consistency and increasing superiority as the children grow older. Although the age at which boys and girls are able to gallop, slide, and skip is approximately the same, girls attain proficiency and a basic pattern in these tasks more rapidly than boys.

These sex differences are often attributed to social influences and to gains of the male in weight and size; these factors are of undoubted importance but the difference especially in throwing is so great and appears so early that one must suspect sex-linked genetic factors not yet understood.

It has been observed that normal children who experience motor problems (low eye-hand efficiency, poor balance, asymmetry, etc.) at age two will usually overcome them; when such problems are found at three they tend to persist in boys more than in girls.

The sex differences found in the movement of young children suggest further study of educational and developmental programs for the preschool and primary years. The really astounding number of dropouts, underachievers, retardates, and delinquents found among school-age boys as compared with girls suggests serious mistakes in our present programs for boys. A study of tastes and trends in early childhood indicates that boys prefer and may especially need a longer period of emphasis on gross movement and a later exposure to sedentary tasks and those requiring fine motor and precise eye-hand coordination than is now offered in our culture.

Teachers and parents should recognize the value of those abilities which the child exhibits (as the gross motor) and help him to use them effectively. In a well-structured program these abilities will be used as stepping stones to develop the confidence, courage, and persistence which will help the child to achieve in other areas.

Race

Data are available for the black and white races; although not conclusive there is some evidence that young children of the black race achieve a higher degree of motor proficiency than white children of the same age (table 12).

Intelligence

It may certainly be assumed that a child's intelligence contributes to his motor learning and thus to his movement abilities. In working with young children two difficulties appear in the assessment of this relationship. First, there is the problem of finding a valid and reliable instrument for testing the intelligence of a child who cannot yet read and write and who has a very limited vocabulary. Second, there exists the probability that much of the child's motor performance at this early age depends upon rapidly maturing neuromuscular patterns resident in the genetic structure, rather than upon learning.

Useful tests are available for appraising the intelligence of young children but psychologists warn that the results must be interpreted with caution and the I.Q.s derived from these scores tend to be unstable. (In the author's study, the tests used were the Peabody Vocabulary Test and the Gesell Copy Forms, for two and three year olds; the Goodenough Draw-a-Man Test, the Peabody Picture Vocabulary Test, and the Gesell Copy Forms, for four year olds; the Metropolitan Reading Readiness Test, for five and six year olds—table 12. Motor scores were based on standards and elements listed in chapter two.)

Persons who work with young children are aware of variations in the way children respond to new situations, in the way they follow directions, and in the way they solve problems; these are considered indicative of the degree of intelligence and are easily observed as one studies children in movement. They are difficult to measure objectively but may account in part for the positive but low correlation which the author and other investigators have found between intelligence (I.Q.) and motor score (table 12).

Reading Readiness

The literature for the last several years has been rife with reports examining the relationship of certain aspects of motor (or perceptual-motor) development with reading ability or those factors presumed to indicate readiness to read. These may be summarized as follows:
1. The results of research are often contradictory—some investigators find a high relationship others do not.
2. There are indications that a significant relationship does exist for some children.
3. It has not been established that this relationship is causal; that is, that poor motor ability causes reading deficiency or vice versa.
4. Those movement characteristics most often reported as related to reading proficiency are balance, dominance (mixed or delayed), and eye-hand efficiency.
5. If, as K.E. Whitehurst[1] and others believe, improvement in any dimension will have positive repercussions in the other dimensions, it is logical to support movement education as important in the total development of the child and thus *indirectly* as an aid to reading and other achievements.

---

[1]Keturah E. Whitehurst, "A Charge to the Conference," *Proceedings of Working Conference on Movement Experiences for Young Children* Farmville, Va.: (Longwood College, Sept. 10-19, 1970), pp. 1-2.

TEACHER'S ESTIMATES OF ACHIEVEMENT

Correlations with motor score and teacher's estimates of achievement are positive at ages three, four, and five but the relationship is highest and statistically significant only at three; it decreases at four and from four to five and five to six (table 12). This may indicate that the teacher places a higher value on motor prowess for the younger children and it may also reflect the older child's increasing ability to communicate through other methods than movement.

INDIVIDUAL DIFFERENCES

Norms can be established for movement development. Development can be described for each age level and yet there is always a problem in grouping children by age, sex, race, intelligence, or in any other way. Each child remains different from every other child in the group —alike in many aspects and yet different in the combination of aspects—and will respond in ways which are uniquely his own.

When the level of movement development is described for a given age it usually represents the mean or average performance of all the subjects studied at that age, and it is probable that no child in the group really conforms in all respects to this description. Thus the performer assumed and described for the performance does not exist in reality. The described performance for each age does represent a norm for the subjects studied for that age and so used offers a criterion of value for all persons concerned with young children.

The descriptions given in chapter two and the mean scores given in table 13 are presented as typical for the age and task except as noted in the text.

PRESCRIPTIVE TEACHING

This term is used here to indicate an individual approach to teaching and implies the following procedures.[2]

1. Observing the child during his performance of whatever he is asked to do Like other skills observation requires attention and practice. Observation should be concentrated on one child at a time; the ob-

---

[2]Sheldon R. Rappaport, "Education or Imprisonment," *Foundation and Practices in Perceptual Motor Learning—A Quest for Understanding*, (Washington, D.C.: American Association for Health, Physical Education, and Recreation, 1201 16th Street, N.W. 20036, 1971), pp. 7-8. (The six procedures listed are from Rappaport; the discussion is the author's.)

server should be specific as to what he is looking for. If the activity observed is complex it should be fractioned into easily recognized units; a chart or record sheet is helpful to use. At the time or as soon as possible after the observation is made it should be recorded and several observations should be made if possible. When properly trained, aides and other helpers may assist with the observations.

Photography, especially video tape and moving pictures, is a great asset to observation as the pictures can be studied at leisure and over and over; in slow-motion, pictures will often reveal what the eye cannot see as the child moves.

2. *Task analysis* An observer must know the tasks in which the child is to engage.

Twenty-five motor tasks have been analyzed as to elements in chapter two. The observer will find it helpful to use the elements in constructing his own observation record forms. The teacher must ask himself such questions as: Is the child ready? Is the equipment suitable? Is the situation safe? What help will be needed? What motivation is needed? How can the task be adjusted to differing abilities?

3. *Understanding the child's response* The observer must be alert in recognizing the child's emotional and social responses but he must also be aware of the child's response in terms of the developmental movement sequence. He should look for the *general movement characteristics* and for those elements which may be considered as clues to basic pattern. In time he will become highly skilled in judging the child's response and in recognizing the child's needs.

4. *Prescribing* The three preceding steps may be thought of as diagnostic and they must be followed by prescription.

The educator might term this "meeting the child's needs" or "determining objectives." It is seldom indeed that a prescription can be made in one medium; the child's developmental needs in movement may be quite specific but these will be linked with home and family, with his peer group, with his state of health and with other factors. The teacher must deal with all of these but as a teacher of movement *and* of children he must be able to give the specific help needed—and recognize the need for it.

5. *Selection of teaching techniques* Of these S. R. Rappaport says:

> These techniques can be listed in a hierarchy, from the least complicated to the most difficult. Then we can try them one at a time and receive feedback information on how each works in helping the child to achieve

that specific objective. If one approach fails then after getting the necessary feedback about it over a period of time additional techniques can be used to achieve the goal.[3]

Such a hierarchy might be involved in teaching a five year old to skip.

a) He may try to skip by following the teacher; if he is able to do so on *one foot only* the teacher will know that he is developing the pattern and will be successful after several days of practice trials.
b) If the child runs without any two-part rhythm he may be returned to the gallop and practice it with both right and left leads for several days before trying the skip again; or—
c) The teacher may take him by the hand and skip with him or—
d) He may be placed between two good "skippers" from whom he may catch the rhythmic pattern.

In using such techniques the teacher or parent should present each one joyfully so that the child will be a zestful participant, uninhibited and free to find his own way. Suitable music, a drum or other percussion will assist the child in adapting his movement to the uneven rhythm.

It is inevitable that the child will experience failure sometimes but he should be protected from the frustration of repeated failure. It is unwise to persist in practicing incorrect patterns of movement. If a child is unsuccessful in a particular task it is usually helpful to expose him to a simpler but related task in which he can reach success. In this way he can practice similar movements and restore his confidence. Halverson has demonstrated that a young child who tries a task repeatedly without success will be so conditioned that he will be unsuccessful in other tasks which he had been able to accomplish previously.[4]

6. *Helping children to independence*   Or as Rappaport puts it "to be boss of one's self."[5]

This is to say that all teaching should be designed to make the individual increasingly independent. The child has social and emotional needs which he must meet and he must interact with others in his group; he must be aware of the rights and reactions of others and the ways in which he can influence them. His feelings, his adaptations, and his behavior must be recognized as his responsibility. It is thus that he

---

[3]Rappaport, in *Foundations and Practices*, p. 8, col. 1.
[4]L. E. Halverson, "Development of Motor Patterns in Young Children," *Quest*, Monograph VI (May 1966), pp. 51-52.
[5]Rappaport, in *Foundations and Practices*, p. 8, col. 2.

learns to take his place in the world as a responsible citizen and as a well-adjusted individual.

These six procedures expressed in various ways have been termed the scientific method. Each procedure may be considered a teaching skill, useful for parents and others who work with young children as well as for teachers. These procedures, although they include task and situational analysis, are definitely child-centered and recognizably difficult to apply if one adult has to work with a large number of young children at one time.

CREATIVITY

Perhaps a reader might infer that the "scientific method" presented above requires a highly structured and predetermined approach to teaching and learning, but it is necessary to understand that creativity is a part of all good teaching and important to easy, comfortable, and useful learning.

The creative teacher is one who can devise an appropriate prescription, discard it, and try another and another; he is one who can accept the child's own level of aspiration and yet envision for him levels beyond this; he is one who can accept a good method or outcome which is the child's but not what the teacher expected. The teacher is creative when he can share with the child his own enthusiasm, his interests, and his vision while leaving the child free to find his own way.

The creative learner is one who learns by discovery rather than by precept. In the early years the child is creative in his learning and learns largely through exploration and discovery. As memory is established and memories build up he achieves a storehouse of data which he can use for reference; at this point he can use experience to make hypotheses and reach new discoveries. With the ability to understand and use speech he can receive information from others—he uses this creatively and makes it his own only when he acts upon it, uses it in some way, and is aware of the results; for example, when mother says warningly to the toddler, "Hot," he extends his hand toward the radiator, feels the heat, says "Hot!" and withdraws his hand. When he grows older and can use books readily he will become able to use information from them creatively, as in problem solving, without physically testing all parts of the method. But even then the learning which becomes his own will be that with which he interacts in some way—by telling it to another, by using it, or by building it into an idea or concept.

The preschooler up to the age of five is very busy learning new ways to move and practicing those he already knows. He can be helped best by being provided opportunity, motivation, encouragement, and a certain degree of protection, and by being allowed full rein for his creativity and discovery.

At five the child will master the basic patterns of all the simpler fundamental tasks and he can now use these as tools in work and play, in combinations which require greater control, and with more speed, force, and precision. Creativity will be demonstrated by new ways of moving, by expressiveness in dance and dramatic play, and by effective decision making. The child will also be discovering and utilizing more mature elements for such fundamental tasks as catching and hitting balls, skipping, sliding, and balance activities, and for other tasks for which the basic patterns are still incomplete.

References

Chaney, Clara M., and Newell C. Kephart. *Motoric Aids to Perceptual Training—Observation Checklists.* Columbus, Ohio: Charles E. Merrill Publishing Co., 1968 (16 pp.).

Cohen, Alan A. "A Dynamic Theory of Vision." *Journal of Developmental Reading* 6, no. 1 (1971): 15-25.

Cratty, Bryant J., and Sister Margaret Mary Martin. *Perceptual Motor Efficiency in Children.* Philadelphia: Lea and Febiger, 1969.

Sinclair, Caroline B. "Ear Dominance in Preschool Children," and "Dominance Patterns of Young Children, a Follow-up Study," *Perceptual and Motor Skills* 26 (1968): pp. 5-10 and 32 (1971): p. 142.

Whitehurst, Keturah E. "A Charge to the Conference." In *Working Conference Proceedings. Virginia Conference on Movement Experiences for Young Children.* Edited by Eleanor Bobbitt. Farmville, Va.: Longwood College, 1970.

chapter six

CASE STUDIES

In this chapter seven case studies will be presented; four of these have been chosen because they are studies of children who are fairly representative of the norms in movement development for the age at which they were studied; they might be spoken of as typical children and yet each child also varies from the norm. The last three cases are presented because they deviate widely from the movement development norms and because in their variations they offer special problems for analysis and help.

CASE NUMBER ONE

Bobby was first observed at the age of 33 months and over a period of two years. He was an attractive looking blonde boy who seemed to adjust well to the nursery school which he had entered about two months previously. His parents were divorced and he and his older brother were both enrolled in the nursery school. His father did not see the family; his mother was employed as an operating-room nurse in a nearby hospital. The children appeared well cared for with good family support. In medical examination Bobby was reported to be of average height and weight and all findings were negative.

66 Movement of the Young Child: Ages Two to Six

When given a psychological examination at the age of 40 months Bobby's mental age was estimated at 4.17 with an I.Q. of 112. The psychologist reported him very responsive with higher performance on gross motor and language items than on visual-fine motor items; she commented that he needed guidance with visual-fine motor competencies.

When a teachers' estimate was compiled at the age of 40 months Bobby was reported as a "roaming and immature child," but he was said to be average in manipulative skill, comprehension, motor performance, creativity, and social adjustment. His health was reported as "good" and he was said to be "good" in self-care.

In two years of study and four periods of filming and recorded observation of movement development, Bobby was reported successively as willing but uncertain, eager and competent, responsive and pleased, and capable and teasing. His self-image seemed positive and he portrayed a pleasing sense of humor. In terms of total motor score Bobby showed some fluctuation when compared with children of his own age but he was still quite close to the mean—0.2, 5.9, and 2.8 above in the first three filming periods at ages 33, 39 and 45 months respectively and 0.7 below the mean at 51 months.

More specifically at age 33 months he was advanced in his age group in ascending stairs, in carrying a weight, in pulling against resistance, and in the standing broad jump from an elevated platform. He was above average in bouncing on the board, in climbing a ladder, in descending stairs and in running. He was below average in creeping and inept in catching a ball, in the forward roll, hitting a ball, pushing, and walking a beam. In other activities Bobby's scores were average for his age group.

At 51 months Bobby had achieved success in all of the twenty-five activities except the figure-8-run, hopping, and skipping—which are customarily achieved later.

When his scores over the four recorded periods are studied it becomes obvious that many scores were higher at 45 months than at 51 months. It is probable that Bobby rises to a challenge but does not always exert his best efforts in familiar and repeated situations.

Bobby was listed as right dominant (hand and foot) though he showed some uncertainty with the kicking foot at age 2. He showed elements of total body assembly in throwing at 2½ and in hitting at both 3 and 3½. Like many children he used an underhand throw at 30 months but readily assumed the overhand form at later ages. He exhibited little "know how" for pulling and pushing, that is, he lost control and used jerky movements, but he was usually successful.

Bobby exhibited varying asymmetries in creeping and never made high scores at this task. He could gallop at age 2 but had not achieved a smooth rhythm at 3½; he could slide to the left at 3 but like many children could not skip or hop at 51 months. Bobby exhibited some opposition of the arms at age 2 when running; later there was occasional asymmetry in the use of the arms and his toes sometimes pointed out in running. Like most children of his age he ran with heel or sole contact rather than with ball-of-foot.

In walking, the body was well aligned though the toes sometimes pointed out.

Bobby was proud of his forward roll which he performed consistently at 30 months and with agility and good direction at 42 months.

Bobby, older than two-thirds of the children in his age group, was slightly above the mean in motor score but he showed considerable fluctuation in scores from task to task, from one trial of a task to another, at different ages and, probably, in response to challenge. It cannot be said that Bobby was an average boy; but it can be said with reasonable assurance that Bobby was a normal boy, developing in a normal way, with a normal need for guidance and direction.

Questions

1. As Bobby's teacher what would be your primary objective in helping him with movement?
2. Would you consider four-part movements such as creeping and climbing important? Why?
3. What might be the special value of symmetrical movements such as the standing broad jump, bouncing on the board, the forward roll?
4. What tasks might help Bobby to point his toes straight ahead? Whose advice might be sought before attempting this correction?
5. Since Bobby can gallop should you teach him the skip and slide *now*?

CASE NUMBER TWO

Janie was first observed at 31 months and over a period of three years. She was large for her age and seemed a little shy. Her father was a medical student and her mother was employed at the medical college nearby. Janie, an only child, appeared to have a happy, well-adjusted home. There were no evidences of ill health and, although large in frame, Janie was not overweight. Her psychological examination at

38 months revealed a mental age of 3.42; an I.Q. of 107. The psychologist reported a tendency toward dismissal in the face of doubt and adherence to her own standards. There appeared to be some sound distortions, particularly in the use of the letters w and l.

When a teacher s estimate was compiled at age 50 months Janie was rated as "good" in self-care, manipulative skills, comprehension, motor performance, creativity, social adjustment, and health.

In the six periods of recorded filming and observation she was described by the observer as stimulated, anxious, diffident and anxious, unsure but adequate, responsive but easily discouraged.

Janie was younger than two-thirds of the children in her age group but taller and a little heavier than most of them. She was right dominant in hand and foot (also ear and eye). In motor score Janie's total average was slightly above that for her group. After the first two recording periods, when her scores were 1.9 *above* and 6 *below* the mean respectively, her scores were consistently above the mean with a range of 0.2 to 6.

At 31 months Janie evidenced average or better proficiency for her age in all motor tasks except catching a ball, the standing broad jump from an elevation, and walking the balance beam. She moved quickly but was stiff and unbalanced in jumping, and sometimes poorly aligned in walking, with toes pointed out and head down. She seemed quite shy. By 49 months she was moving more confidently.

At 37 months Janie was proficient in catching; at 43 months she had attained success in the jump and walking the balance beam, but she did not forge ahead in these or in throwing, then or later, as she did in many other tasks. She could slide at 41 months and with both right and left leads at 53, skip at 49 months, and consistently attained a maximum score in galloping after 49 months.

Janie used opposition in the run at 43 months but inconsistently then and thereafter. She was able to hop on the right foot at 43 months and on the left at 61 months.

In hitting a ball Janie did not use a true sideward stance until 61 months and weight transfer and body rotation were used only slightly if at all. Janie's creeping and climbing lacked rhythm and symmetry. In climbing and ascending stairs the right foot led, while in descending the leading foot was the left; this reversal is customary for most children with the preferred (dominant) foot leading in ascent and giving support in descent.

At the age of 3 Janie began to close her eyes and turn her head when a ball was thrown to her; at 4 she seemed to find a weight of twelve pounds very taxing for carrying.

This young child was greatly concerned when she felt that she was not achieving according to expectations; she responded well to encouragement and help but was alarmed at even small indications of pressure. Her inconsistencies in progress might be attributed to her sensitive emotional response, but might also be due to the day to day variations which can be expected of any happy, healthy, normal child.

Questions
1. In what tasks did Janie appear most advanced?
2. In what tasks did she appear least advanced?
3. As you compare her achievement with that of Bobby *at the same age* do you find differences which appear typical of boys and girls?
4. Since Janie, at 61 months, has made little progress toward acquiring total body assembly for speed, would you recommend prescriptive action?
5. Design a task or series of tasks which will promote total body assembly in hitting or throwing.

CASE NUMBER THREE

Bruce was first observed at 49 months and over a period of three years. He was a handsome blonde child with two sisters, one older and the other less than a year old. His father had died recently. On his first day at nursery school Bruce did not wish to stay and wept despondently and then angrily; his mother dealt with him kindly but firmly. He soon adjusted and was revealed to be a happy child; he was the second youngest in his age group. Bruce's mother remarried after two years and a new baby was born to this marriage. After the first two years of the study, during which Bruce was enrolled in a public school program (at ages 4 and 5), he attended a private church school.

When Bruce was given a medical examination at 52 months his visual acuity was found to be normal but there was muscle weakness of the left eye. Other findings were negative though some immaturity of body alignment was noted. The mother reported a later ophthalmological examination in which the physician did not recommend treatment. When tested at 51 months Bruce was found to have a mental age of 5.75 and an I.Q. of 133. At age 5 Bruce was tested for an I.Q. of 124 which was the highest in a special "follow-through" group of twelve children. At this point he rated low normal on the Metropolitan Reading Readiness Test but was considered up to age expectancy by his teacher. A teacher's estimate secured in March of his year in first grade (age 78 months) rated him "good" in reading. He was reported to be very alert and interested, good in phonics and in number concepts and skills.

At 49 months Bruce appeared physically immature with soft flesh, protruding abdomen, and somewhat infantile gait; he was able to achieve motor scores comparable to or better than other children in his age group. Though younger than most, his mean score was within 0.9 of the mean for all children of his age group, and for three of the five recording periods available his scores were 0.5 to 10.1 above the mean. There was considerable fluctuation as he fell to 18.4 below the mean at the third recording period. His performance in hitting and catching balls was especially erratic as was also his performance in hopping and skipping. He achieved average or better success in other motor tasks with occasional fluctuations.

Bruce was found to be consistently right (for hand, foot, eye, and ear) in part preference or dominance.

In four successive periods of observation Bruce was described as zestful, usually smooth in performance, exuberant, assured and direct.

In kindergarten at age 5 Bruce walked with beautiful erectness and symmetry; he could hop on either foot and was successful in walking the two-inch beam but was uncertain of balance when landing from a jump. His jumping ability was average (15 and 18 inches in the high jump at 61 and 67 months, and 34½ and 39 inches in the standing broad). Bruce was one of the few who accelerated the broad jump by moving his legs forward in flight, but he did not use this characteristic consistently; he was also inconsistent in the timing of the arms with the jump.

The time in the run was better than average but Bruce did not lift his knees nor did he contact with the ball-of-foot though a few of his classmates did.

Bruce's gallop and slide were easy and rhythmic at age 5 but he could skip on only one foot; the true skip was attained at 67 months but performed with effort and tension.

In throwing and hitting a ball Bruce's control was poor but there was some semblance of total body assembly including transfer of weight and body rotation. He used a forward stance in throwing but not in batting.

Bruce ran the figure-8 course without error though slowly; he was able to do both forward and backward rolls but did not roll to his feet.

In the first few months of first grade Bruce was able to jump (42 inches) and throw (50 feet) greater distances than before but his patterns of movement showed little change though greater consistency.

He was able to use body-rotation more effectively in hitting. Some tasks he performed less competently than at age 5; for example, he pushed and pulled with great competence the previous year and did not maintain momentum in these tasks at age 6, and his running time was slower than at 5.

Questions
1. What are the positive factors in Bruce's life as related in his case history?
2. List the negative factors.
3. Does Bruce's motor development at age 5 appear to be satisfactory? Support your answer.
4. What factors in Bruce's case study indicate that he needs help? Suggest one or more procedures.
5. List three or more bits of information which would be pertinent to the above questions and which are not given in the case study.

CASE NUMBER FOUR

Shirley was first observed at 52 months and over a three-year period. She was a slender, pretty child, rather fragile in appearance. She was the fifth of seven children with five brothers, three older, and one sister less than two years older than Shirley. This sister, Betty, seemed quite protective of the younger child. The father was employed irregularly but later secured a steady job. The two girls appeared malnourished and anxious but seemed to be less so as the family situation improved. When Shirley was to receive a medical examination at 42 months she became so upset that the examination was not completed. At 54 months the physician reported a low-grade infection of the left eye which cleared up later. There were no other positive findings.

Psychological testing at 57 months found a mental age of 5.50 and an I.Q. of 112. The psychologist commented favorably on Shirley's sense of humor.

Shirley was reported a low scorer on the reading readiness test at age 5 and in March of her first-grade year her teacher reported slow but steady progress; at this time her reading and other abilities were said to be below grade level.

In five periods of observation at intervals of six months Shirley was described successively as fluid in movement, poised, having accurate focus and output, and confident and caring. She tested mixed in dominance, right in hand and foot and left in eye and ear.

Shirley ranked tenth in age in her own age group of nineteen students. Her mean of motor scores was slightly better (0.5) than the mean of the group. After the first observation and recording periods, in which she exhibited both babyish behavior and much anxiety, her scores ranged from 0.4 to 3.6 above the mean for the group. In the first period she was 7 points below the mean. After this first period she was consistent in her performance of motor tasks though at times she seemed fearful of failure or of embarrassment before the group.

In kindergarten Shirley could hop easily on either foot and had no trouble in moving from a 4-inch to the 2-inch walking beam. Shirley was proficient and rhythmic in bouncing a large ball; she kicked a ball with fair success but poor control. In throwing and hitting she did not use a sideward stance, and transfer of weight and body rotation were lacking (distance of the throw was 28 feet 7 inches).

Shirley's movements were well integrated and symmetrical in creeping and climbing. Her carriage was excellent in walking and at other times except when she became self-conscious. Her total body assembly was good for carrying, pushing, and pulling.

At age 5 Shirley's time for the 50-foot run was 3.8 seconds; her high jump was 20 inches, but she did not accentuate her arm lift; in the standing broad jump of 30 inches she used some leg thrust in flight. She was not able to follow the figure-8 course accurately. Her gallop, slide, and skip were competent but she could not start the pattern of the slide without a demonstrator.

In first grade Shirley evidenced some tension and loss of movement quality which was noticeable in pushing, in the forward roll, in sliding, in skipping, and in kicking a ball. She employed a sideward stance and better total body assembly in throwing and batting, and she began to use a ball-of-foot contact in running.

Questions

1. What are Shirley's greatest physical needs?
2. If any of these have to do with movement how would you help her meet them?
3. Could you help with other needs? How?
4. What are Shirley's greatest psychological needs?
5. What assets does she have which might be utilized in meeting these psychological needs?

CASE NUMBER FIVE

Douglas was first observed at 50 months and over a period of three years. He was the youngest of four children and his parents were divorced. At one time Douglas was living with his grandmother and his mother's address was unknown but then the mother returned and took all of the children to a new home. At 50 months Douglas, a small black boy with good features and large sad eyes, was the fourth youngest in his age group of nineteen students. He was always clean and neatly dressed. Even though he seemed quiet and rather unresponsive at this age, his medical examination at 55 months revealed no positive findings.

Douglas was tested at 54 months and found to have a mental age of 2.83. The corresponding I.Q. was given as below 75. The psychologist commented that Douglas was left-handed and that there seemed to be a dysfunction in coordinating motor function with sensory experience.

During the first two periods of observation this child was hesitant and immature in movement, receiving motor scores of 3.5 and 10.6 below the means for his group. He did indeed appear left-handed but used his right foot in kicking (usually children kick with the right foot if right-handed and with the left foot if left-handed). At 56 months he was still descending stairs foot-over-foot. His balance was poor. He seemed dreamy and abstracted; the psychologist expressed some doubt as to his status in a group of normally intelligent children.

In the following summer Douglas' family moved to a new home in an urban-development area. When next observed, Douglas was attending a larger, all-black school in which the staff was composed of both white and black teachers. At once the observer noted that Douglas seemed more alert and responsive; he followed directions well; his motor skills had improved. Although still among the youngest in his group his motor score was 12.8 above the mean. In successive recording periods (in the last half of kindergarten and the first semester of first grade) he scored 13.2 and 11.5 above the means respectively. During this time, he became consistent in the preference of his right hand and left foot. In earlier testing he was recorded as left dominant in eye and ear; later tests revealed him to be left-eyed and right-eared. In four observations spaced at six-month intervals Douglas was described as slow in response, becoming highly efficient, controlled and focused, unsure but persistent.

In kindergarten Douglas tested average or above in balance and all movement tasks. His teacher reported him doing well in school at this time. His reading readiness score was one of the two highest in his group of eighteen students. In first grade the teacher's estimate of reading ability was "average." He was rated "good" in social adjustment and his achievement was said to be continuous and satisfactory.

Questions
1. What are the factors in Douglas' history which you find of special interest?

2. What further investigation do you suggest for this child?
3. If he were to experience considerable retrogression in second grade (which he did both in school achievement and social adjustment) what procedure would you recommend?
4. If the teacher reported "not living up to his potential" how would you interpret this with reference to information available?
5. Are referrals indicated?

CASE NUMBER SIX

George was 39 months old when first observed and it was his second year in the nursery school. Observation continued for three years. His parents were separated and his mother refused to give any information about the father. An only child, he lived with his mother who was young and pretty and had a secretarial position in a physician's office. As problems developed the mother seemed resistant to them and unwilling to refer her son for help.

George was a disruptive child in a group and he frequently hit, pulled, or pinched the other children. His appearance was attractive when he was well groomed but his clothes were usually too large and sometimes they were shabby or soiled. He was most responsive when alone with an adult, and in his three years of nursery school he was often separated from the other children for special tasks.

There were no positive findings in George's medical examination. In the psychological examination at 46 months George recorded a mental age of 3.83 and an I.Q. of 97. The psychologist commented that he adhered to his own standard but frequently changed his response; he kept touching the examination items.

His teachers at the nursery school rated George "average" in self-care, manipulative skill, comprehension, creativity, and social adjustment. He was rated "good" in health and "poor" in motor performance, and he was said to be uncooperative.

In the third year of observation George was enrolled in a public school for kindergarten and for after-school care. In the preceding summer his mother had married a young man whose work included public relations and TV programs. George spoke of his new father with pride and was pleased with the acclaim he (George) received when he appeared on a local TV show. However, his behavior continued to be disruptive and hostile to other children. At this time, he received special attention from a kind and wise teacher, from the school principal, and from the guidance director.

Although this child appeared strong, well, and intelligent, his motor scores were consistently below the means for his age group. The range below the mean was from 1.8 to 15.8 with a mean deviation of -10.1. The deviation tended to be greater as the child grew older.

George was consistently right dominant. In five observations over 2½ years, he was described as jerky and eager, over- and undertrying (at three successive observations spaced over eighteen months), and growing in skill and assurance.

In approaching the motor tasks and in his success with them, George was inconsistent. Sometimes he seemed to try very hard and with much tension—at other times he appeared to seek failure as when he would run through a bar instead of trying to jump it. His scores were, of course, erratic. He was poor in all balance activities and especially backward in hopping; he was unable to skip and his galloping and sliding were delayed. His catching, hitting, and kicking were spasmodic and his throwing was babyish until the age of 5. At age 5 he was still using a foot-over-foot pattern in descending stairs. At all ages he showed asymmetry in movement, especially noticeable in the oppositional use of the arms in running. At all ages his pattern of creeping was distorted and irregular.

George was recognized as an emotional and behavioral problem early in nursery school. Various efforts were made to help him but the mother refused to recognize any problem except that of his immediate behavior which she felt should be dealt with on the spot. As George grew older he became more aware of his deficiencies in movement. The observer usually worked with him alone because he was more responsive and exhibited less tension. He appeared to enjoy the movement tasks but sometimes distorted his performance purposefully.

Questions

1. List the special problems which George seems to have.
2. Analyze and criticize the program described or indicated for George in the nursery school.
3. In dealing with George's motor problems do you recommend a direct approach? Explain and give examples.
4. What referrals do you suggest if any? Explain.
5. What are the assets which George has and how may these be used most effectively to help him solve his problems?

CASE NUMBER SEVEN

Kate was first observed at 38 months and over a three-year period. She was tall for her age with beautiful red hair and the brown eyes and pink and white skin which go with it so well. Kate was an only child with divorced parents. She lived with her mother and grandmother and did not see her father. At the nursery school in which Kate was enrolled her mother was spoken of as being overprotective of Kate. The mother was employed as a typist and usually held two jobs so that she had little time with her child, but her affection and concern were continuously expressed.

Kate's medical record revealed a recent tonsilectomy and frequent absences from school. Some of these were due to minor illnesses, others to family emergency or convenience. Kate's speech was unclear and very rapid; some sounds were distorted and she had difficulty in communication, especially if she were excited—which she frequently was.

At 57 months Kate was given psychological tests. Her I.Q. was found to be 67; her developmental age was estimated as 4.00. The psychologist commented on severe sound distortions and misunderstanding of fast verbal directions. Needs were evidenced for emotional closeness and for acceptable channels for energy.

In the second year of observation Kate's mother moved to Florida, but she was not pleased with her life there so she returned to her home city at the end of the year, and Kate was reenrolled in the nursery school for her kindergarten year. Teachers' estimates during kindergarten rated Kate as "average" in self-care, manipulative skill, comprehension, motor performance, creativity, and social adjustment; she was estimated to be "good" in health.

Kate was consistently right dominant in all aspects.

In three widely separated periods of observation Kate was described as erratic, exerting effort, and responding lightly (as though not completely involved).

Kate was consistently below the mean for her age group in motor score; she varied from 9.9 below the norm at 38 months to 16.2 below at 68 months. Her ball handling skills were poor and she was lacking in balance, eye-hand efficiency and symmetry of movement. Her attention span was short and she was easily distracted. She sought attention and was often impulsive in beginning a task without understanding it. Her excessive tension was manifested in rigidity of the hands and fingers, in facial distortion, and in unusual postures.

Kate was described by the observer as tense and unsure, as impulsive and overactive. Her speech problems showed little improvement from ages 3 to 5.

Questions

1. What is your prediction of school success for this child?
2. What help should be made available to her *now*?
3. What help can her teacher give her?
4. How should her mother be advised?
5. Can she be helped through a movement program? How?

References

Cohen, Dorothy H., "The Young Child: Learning to Observe—Observing to Learn." In *The Significance of the Young Child's Motor Development*, pp. 35-44, Washington, D.C.: National Association for the Education of Young Children, 1971.

Halverson, Lolas E., "The Young Child—The Significance of Motor Development." In *The Significance of the Young Child's Motor Development*, pp. 17-31, Washington, D.C.: National Association for the Education of Young Children, 1971.

Simpson, Dorothy M. *Learning to Learn*. Columbus, Ohio: Charles E. Merrill Publishing Co., 1968.

chapter seven

SPACE, TIME, AND EQUIPMENT

Since the child learns through interaction with the world around him, the elements of his environment, his exposure to them, and their arrangement within his surroundings are of the utmost importance. If the child learns best through discovery, exploration, and experience then his environment must be stimulating, appropriate to his needs and abilities, and reasonably safe. If movement, and especially gross vigorous movement, is essential for development and especially important for the nervous system, then the environment must provide generously for such movement in space, time, and equipment.

SPACE

When the infant graduates from bassinet to crib, from crib to playpen, and from playpen to living room or nursery, he is adjusting to increasing dimensions of space. After the playpen he shares his space with others, and when he has early and frequent excursions into family living areas and to outdoors, this adjustment to space sharing comes gradually, easily, and with joy. As the child becomes larger and more mobile, his space requirements grow. Urban living is not conducive to space but fortunate indeed is the young child who has indoor play space in his home and a large yard for play.

In nursery schools and day care centers space is a *must* both indoors and out. A standard of thirty-five square feet per child is suggested for indoor space. It should be so arranged that each child has at least one permanent space which is his own; this may be a cubicle in which he keeps his wraps and his other possessions; it should provide a seat which is strictly his and which may be used as his special refuge. In addition there should be other spaces which are his own at times—a cot or mat for resting, a seat at the table for meal time or snacks, a mat or rug for certain activities; these help in giving a child a feeling of security and they also assist in orderly movement and foster freedom within acceptable boundaries. Later the child can work from a space represented by a mark on the floor, and still later from his "own space" which has no visible boundaries but from which he will not encroach on the space of others.

The indoor space which is shared by all children should be large enough and uncluttered so that all may move freely though with recognition of the rights of others (this the children must learn!). It is desirable to have some equipment for vigorous physical activity indoors but it should not be installed if it causes undue restriction of space. When "centers" of various kinds are established (e.g., housekeeping, shop, reading, music,) one for climbing, balance beam, mat activities, bean bags, etc., should be included. There should always be one large open space (or one from which chairs and tables may be easily moved) so that in inclement weather the children may move actively together.

The outdoor space should be generous with appropriate areas of sun and shade. Trees, shrubs, flowers, and water (a brook or small pool) offer a rich and attractive learning environment. For some occasions "his own space" may be provided by a sturdy mat or rug which is taken to the playground. "Shared space" is provided with fixed equipment and by areas for special activities—there may be one for "digging," another for tricycle riding, a third for climbing and balancing on equipment set up for this purpose, and others. The outdoor space must be so shaped and arranged that children have the opportunity to run *fast* on a straightaway. Only thus will they get the proper stimulation for oppositional use of arms and legs. Opposition, started in creeping and climbing and developed from age three primarily through running, is the basis for the highly integrated use of the body which we have called total body assembly. A distance of at least eighty feet should be allowed for a run at top speed and a slow-down which insures safety and avoids a fence, building, or street. The number of activity centers on the playground should allow for active participation by all children in

Simple equipment can be used indoors.

Photograph from the Child Development Laboratory, School of Home Economics, University of Missouri, Columbia, Missouri

groups of four or five. There should also be sufficient open space for brief participation by a large number of children in selected activities.

Safety is of course a primary consideration in arranging space both indoors and out. It is usual in public schools to provide a fenced area of the playground for the smaller children. This is desirable but it should be located near the classroom with controlled access.

Everyone is susceptible to the stimulation of space. The traveler is excitedly aware of the expanse of the ocean, the open sweep of the prairie, or the vastness of the universe seen in flight. Children respond with ecstasy and exuberance to the shimmering space of an empty gymnasium, to the smooth greenness of a hockey or football field, or to the charms of an open meadow. They may be overexcited by the size and by the potentialities for moving and for exploration, but their exposure to a big space constitutes a worthwhile "field trip" in which they may learn much about space and about themselves.

OTHER ENVIRONMENTAL CONSIDERATIONS

Water

Wading and swimming opportunities are highly desirable for small children. The facilities present special problems of supervision and

82 Movement of the Young Child: Ages Two to Six

maintenance. If there is a brook or spring on the property it might be wise to maintain it so that the children can use it. Lacking this, a practical method is to provide a sturdy, portable, plastic pool which can be used from time to time and which can be easily cleaned and filled. For its selection, use, and maintenance the advice of the local department of public health should be sought.

Water play may also be encouraged with tubs and buckets of water; plants can be watered, wells can be dug, boats can be made and sailed. Children who enjoy water play usually learn to swim easily and are ready for instruction in classes at ages six or seven. They will swim earlier than this if encouraged, and taught or supervised individually.

Water play has many forms and values.

If a pool or other good swimming facility is available great benefits may be derived from it. Trips may be taken to a nearby pool, lake, or beach. Usually the water is deeper than necessary for such small children and therefore one adult to every two children or even a one-to-one ratio may be necessary. Young children should be allowed to move slowly in their acquaintance with big water. The American Red Cross provides excellent materials for the "preswimmer."

Surfacing

Floors for young children's classrooms and play activities should be smooth, sealed, and clean. Wood is preferred over other surfaces because it is more resilient; tile placed over wood is satisfactory; concrete slabs are not sufficiently resilient and concrete should not be used unless a wood floor with sills is placed over it. Resiliency of the floor is important for the protection of small bones and joints.

A large rug is highly desirable for the classroom. It should be of short nap and easily cleaned. It may be used in many ways—for protection in floor play; as a good, and quiet, surface for wheeled and rolling toys; for warmth on chilly days; as a center for stories, music, and other sit-on-the floor activities.

For outdoor space a large, level, grassy area is highly desirable. If the space is adequate the grass will not wear badly except around the fixed equipment; these areas may be covered with weatherproof mats, outdoor carpeting, or shallow sand pits. Jungle gyms, climbing poles, acting bars, and slides should have mats or sand pits for landing; if the surfacing beneath them is made of concrete or asphalt it should be replaced or heavily padded. For these areas grass might be adequate but it soon wears away.

Smaller outdoor areas may be surfaced with quick drying material and used when the grass is wet. These areas (thirty feet by sixty feet perhaps) should be placed close to the exits from the classrooms. It is recommended that they be built of one of the resilient surfaces rather than asphalt or concrete. There are several preparations of these materials on the market; installation is rather expensive but they are durable and can be maintained at low cost; moreover they are relatively nonabrasive and lessen the injuries from falls and tumbles.

Clothing

For best movement development clothing should be light and nonrestrictive. Children are often burdened with thick heavy coats which make quick, vigorous movement difficult. Materials are now available for outdoor clothing which are warm, light, and water repellent. Warm clothing for outdoor play is essential for cold weather; it should provide covering for the legs and head; mittens or gloves may be fastened through the sleeves with cords. Boots or overshoes are sometimes needed for outdoor play and especially when there is snow on the ground. Outdoor clothing should be roomy but not so large as to be bunglesome.

It is advisable to keep a lighter wrap at the center or school so that the child can wear it if the weather is warmer at midday or use it as an extra wrap should the weather become colder after he leaves home.

Clothing should not be so tight as to be restrictive but it may also be restrictive if it is too large. The small boy who is always "hitching up" his too-loose belt and/or trousers will be hampered in his running. Nor can he run fast if the jeans are too long and fall around his ankles.

Clothes may be pretty and attractive but they should also be durable and suitable for doing things; knit materials are easily maintained, "give" for free movement, and are available in many colors and styles. Extra clothes should be available at the center or school so that a change is possible when spills and other accidents to clothing occur.

In the British schools small children wear shorts for active play; the girls wear thin shirts of our T-shirt variety, and the boys are bare-torsoed. This has not been customary in America but certainly our children should be less hampered by clothing than many of them are; if clothing were lighter and more clinging we would be able to observe the developing movement of children more closely, and they would be able to move with greater ease.

Shoes merit special consideration; boys' shoes tend to be heavy and stiff, robbing the small muscles of the feet of their needed development. Some shoes, especially some sandals, offer little protection and do not give the support needed if the child is constantly on hard surfaces. High boots, especially those made of plastic, may bind and hamper circulation; they also tend to trap moisture and prevent good ventilation. Unless the pediatrician advises otherwise, shoes for young children should be light, flexible, roomy but well fitted; they should offer mild support without being restrictive. They should be made of leather or heavy cloth and the linings should be smooth; if the sole is rubber there should be an inner lining. A laced shoe stays on well and can be adjusted to the child's foot. Shoes and socks should be discarded before they are binding or too short. The bare foot may pick up disease or be injured by tacks, broken glass, or other debris, but on a clean and resilient surface such as grass, sand, or carpet, a barefooted child has much greater use of his feet than when he is wearing shoes. Perhaps at home, perhaps in special areas, each child can have some barefoot activity every day; in this way he may be helped to develop and retain the strength and flexibility of the feet so important for comfort through the years.

TIME

A young child is, by nature, exceedingly active. At age two if you ask him to come to you he will run; at three he may walk because he has been taught to do so, but if he has his choice he will run. Our culture places severe restrictions on the mobility of children. They learn not to get on the floor, not to climb on the furniture, not to run in the house. And yet most of them spend at least twenty of every twenty-four hours indoors. In addition they are restricted by stiff shoes and clothing which is often bunglesome, heavy, and tight.

In suggesting time requirements for movement, it is well to think first of time out of doors. The magic of being outdoors is not completely understood; it includes sun, fresh air (we hope!), growing things, grass underfoot (hopefully), and blue sky overhead; it may also include rain in the face (when properly clad), puddles to wade in (when booted or barefoot) and the beauty and charm of snow. But certainly the out of doors also includes freedom in its magic—freedom beyond that of four walls, a ceiling overhead, a certain and unchanging floor underneath, and familiar furnishings.

So time must be allowed for outdoor living. This must vary with the weather but each program for preschoolers should be planned for long outdoor sessions, totaling not less than half of the school day, and not less than four hours in at least two sessions for day care of seven hours or more.

If the outdoors is appropriately set up and space and equipment are provided, most young children will engage in rather vigorous movement interspersed with brief periods of quiet play and rest. But good leadership is essential to insure that there is a fair distribution of opportunity, that timid and less active children are encouraged and stimulated, and that appropriate challenge is provided for both the more advanced children and those who tend to lag in movement development. In other words, the teacher must see to the movement experience and development of each child; it is not enough just to provide the opportunity.

It is more difficult to provide for the vigorous activity needs of young children when weather or other conditions limit the use of the playground. To do this indoors requires careful planning. It may be necessary to schedule several groups on a rotating basis for an indoor play area; or it may be necessary for small groups to rotate within the classroom in the use of certain equipment or for a special activity; for brief periods all of the children in a classroom may participate together; this requires forethought and the time interval must be adjusted to the age and interest span of the children. For two year olds and younger three year olds one or two simple motor tasks might be sufficient; for children in the older four- and five-age bracket, group activity might be successful for a period of twenty minutes—seldom longer unless there is a sharp change of pace or focus. For full-day programs indoors, vigorous activity should be offered at least four times during the day; for shorter programs indoors two or three times may be sufficient.

EQUIPMENT

This section will be restricted to equipment used by children in gross movement and to that which seems to have special significance for the development of total body movement. It will be presented in three sections: criteria for proper selection; equipment related to a variety of purposes; and a list of basic equipment for movement development.

Criteria

For the past few years the market has been crowded with "educational" equipment and "learning kits" for younger children. What are the best criteria for selection?

Wisdom dictates and experience confirms the following:

1. Equipment should be sturdy and durable.

2. Equipment should be easy to maintain—washable or otherwise easy to clean, rustproof, and chipproof.

3. Equipment should be safe—no sharp edges, no lead paint, splinterproof, nonflammable.

4. Equipment should be simple—easy to put together and take apart, few parts to be lost.

5. Equipment should be compact and easy to store—parts should fit together, perhaps come apart, covers should be provided when necessary.

6. Equipment should lend itself to purpose—in other words equipment should be selected for the use to be made of it.

7. Equipment should be versatile—that is, 1) equipment is more valuable if it can be used for several purposes and 2) equipment is more valuable if it can be adapted for use in various ways.

Space, Time, and Equipment 87

8. Equipment should be readily available. Much expensive equipment is rarely used because it cannot be left on the playground and space indoors is limited. Every playground for small children should have adjacent to it a safe storage area with large doors in which equipment may be stored; it can then be moved easily to and from the play area.
9. Good storage areas should be provided in or adjacent to the classroom or indoor play area.
10. Much equipment should be light enough and so constructed that small children can move it from storage area to play space.
11. Playground security should permit the leaving of some equipment (usually fixed) out of doors. This equipment should be weatherproofed with paint or other finish; sandboxes should be covered and locked. Pools, if provided, should be covered and locked.

Pipes and culverts offer new ventures.

Purposeful Use

Equipment should be selected purposefully—for what it will do for the children and for what they can do with it. Equipment is discussed here under nine headings with special reference to the purposes for which it may best be used.

1. Creeping and other floor movement Large flexible tubes which are collapsible have been recommended for creeping practice. Children do enjoy these but their surface and texture are not as conducive to

88   Movement of the Young Child: Ages Two to Six

good oppositional and synchronous movement of the limbs as is a smooth or carpeted floor. Concrete or ceramic culverts are very desirable and may be used by children for creeping and in a variety of other ways. When the knees are used a great deal on the floor or other hard surfaces kneepads held on with ties or an elastic band are recommended. Two year olds are often quite proficient creepers but many have poorly coordinated creeping patterns, and most children have been observed to improve after age 2½ up to age 4. It is probable that floor play should be offered all children until 4 or after.

Rolls, balance activities, and stunts of various kinds are done on the floor which is usually padded for the purpose. A thick carpet, a pillow, a small pad or rug is sufficient for small children. Individual rugs or mats are very useful. They may be color coded for groups or marked with individual names or symbols. The mats should be small enough and light enough for the children to move them easily. The children should be taught to keep the mats clean.

2. Climbing   Fixed climbing equipment such as a jungle gym should be provided out of doors. This should be large enough to accommodate six to ten children and should provide one or more ladder-like areas, bars to swing from about four feet from the ground, and a soft area underneath for landing.

In addition other ladders should be provided which may be fixed at strategic spots (as for slides, grape arbors, etc.) or with hooks so that they may be moved from place to place but can be well stabilized. Children should be encouraged to climb; it is exceedingly developmental because all parts of the body are involved, and it is also ego-enhancing. However, climbing is potentially dangerous and requires stable equipment and supervision.

3. Opposition   Creeping and climbing require the use of opposition of the limbs in a series of four-point support positions. This method is also used in a somewhat different fashion in swimming, but seldom otherwise for locomotion after the child gains ready mobility in the erect position. The need for space for a straight run has been emphasized. The various games of tag, obstacle races, and the crowded playgrounds themselves foster evasive or broken field running but this is not very conducive to smooth opposition of the limbs. Brisk walking, with the hands and arms free, promotes opposition as do other activities which require little or no equipment. For learning to go up and down stairs, stairways (not less than five steps) should be provided. Real stairs may also be used if available and of suitable size. A short journey to use a real stairway is an interesting learning experience for three and four year olds who do not have stairways in their homes or schools.

4. *Balance*   All activities in the erect position are balance developing activities for very young children. Learning to stand and move without support requires the infant's greatest efforts until age two or after. He gets many falls and abrupt sit-downs but soon summons the will to try again and again. Walking and running are balance trials for the toddler; hopping, skipping, and sliding constitute balance challenges for the three and four year olds. The walking beam, the balance board, the bounce board, tricycles, bicycles, roller and ice skates—these and many other pieces of equipment can be used progressively to develop a greater sense of balance. They are challenging, interesting, and lend themselves to infinite variations. Tumblers, divers, horseback riders, dancers, and fliers must have keenly developed senses of balance and direction. The development of balance seems to occur to a marked degree in early childhood.

5. *Rhythm*   Rhythm is an integral part of all movement and has visual, auditory, tactile, and very strong kinesthetic components.

Rhythm has been defined as repetition of an accent.[1] Walking, running, and hopping are movements of even rhythm in which the intervals between accents are the same; an exception would be the limping walk of a person with an injured foot. Galloping, sliding, and skipping are two-part forms of locomotion in which the rhythm recurs in short-long (or long-short) couplets. The waltz and two-step have three-part patterns—the waltz even, the two-step uneven; and there are four and five-part patterns also. The rhythm of a person creeping may be four-part in which each limb is moved at a different time (as *RH, LF, LH, RF*) which is the more elementary pattern, or two-part (*RH* and *LF, LH* and *RF*). The two-part homolateral pattern (*LH* and *LF, RH* and *RF*) is often observed in the early creeper but rarely persists in the normal child after age two.

Steps and ladder rungs should be spaced so that short legs can move easily and rhythmically. Bounce boards and swings help children develop, experience, and enjoy rhythmic movement. Rhythmic movement can be soothing or it can be intensely exciting; the wise teacher uses it for both purposes. The piano, recorded music, and simple instruments which the children can use will be of help in developing rhythm and rhythmic movement.

---

[1]Clarence L. Barnhart, ed. *Comprehensive Desk Dictionary* (Garden City, N.Y.: Doubleday and Co. Inc., 1962), p. 667.

6. Ball handling Balls are probably the most universal of all playthings. They are used in every country and by every people. They are used in the play of young children and in the lifetime sports so popular with adults of varying ages; they are essential equipment for the "great games" of our country—baseball, football, and basketball. Balls can be used in many ways—they can be rolled, tossed, bowled, thrown, hit, and kicked; they can be blocked, volleyed, caught, trapped, dribbled, or juggled. They can be directed at targets or propelled for distance. They can be used in simple competition as in a throw for distance or in very complex competitive situations like baseball. Balls, typically round, may have other shapes (as a football) and vary greatly in surface, size, and weight.

For young children ball handling requires little equipment except the balls themselves. These should be of at least two sizes—large balls (6 or 8 inches in diameter) and small balls (2½ or 3 inches in diameter). These balls are used for rolling, throwing, catching, kicking, and sometimes for hitting. For hitting, croquet balls (wooden), old (soft) softballs, and tennis balls are satisfactory. Croquet mallets (with shortened handles), paddles (similar to paddles for paddle tennis), and small bats made of wood or plastic may be used.

In the interests of safety all hitting should be done in one direction, children must be well apart, and practice might best be in small groups.

Batting tees are very well adapted to the use of small children since they offer stable targets and can be easily adjusted for height.

Children should be allowed a choice and if necessary experimentation in batting right- or left-handed; the use of an established batter's box will help to develop a proper sideward batting stance.

To encourage good distance throwing lanes may be used (to get straight throws) and when a target is reached it may be moved away gradually to encourage more and more use of all body parts in sequence (total body assembly).

The children should have the use of a large ball for each two children and a small ball for each child. Beanbags are useful indoors and to eliminate rolling for very young children. Soft balls of cloth or sponge rubber may also be useful. Light perforated plastic balls will not travel far and are safe to use indoors or when outdoor space is restricted.

7. Resistance activities Boys and girls grow stronger by exposing their muscles to demanding tasks. If a growing boy or girl never attempts a task beyond the strength of a three year old, he will be a weakling all of his life. Small children will push, pull, tug, and drag in varied and persistent ways in order to move objects; frequently they will refuse offered help because the child wants to do it *himself*.

The young child needs objects to push, pull, carry, and lift. Wagons, sleds, and wheelbarrows may be loaded and used as transports. Building, especially with large blocks, bricks, stones, beams, and boards, offers developmental and creative employment. Agricultural projects involving digging, raking, planting, and weeding combine many and varied developmental opportunities. Sawing, hammering, and modeling provide constructive experiences which may offer or combine with tasks which require the economical use of the small child's strength. Bars fastened strongly at different heights will be used by children for all kinds of suspension activities; hanging, chinning, traveling by hand, swinging, and turning (skinning the cat) all require the use and development of arms and shoulders. Ladders may be suspended horizontally and used similarly and by more children.

Care must be used to see that loads are not too heavy, that taxing tasks are not too long pursued, and that strength is utilized to good advantage. The wise leader can do much to help the young child build lifetime attitudes of courage, persistence, and willingness to try.

8. *Power activities* Jumping is a power activity—so called because it results from a tremendous effort exerted through a system of levers all activated simultaneously (or nearly so). When maximum effort is exerted as in competitive jumping, the arms always lead the action in order to overcome their inertia or dead weight at the moment of the takeoff and leg drive. Force will be exerted downward simultaneously by the extension from flexion of hip, knee, ankle, and forefoot (flexion of toes) acting together. The angle of takeoff will vary with the desired flight of the jump—whether it be forward-upward for distance (as in the long or broad jump) or vertical as in the high jump and basketball toss.

Children can jump *down* before they are able to propel the body weight upward. This is fortunate as the child thus experiences takeoff, flight, and landing in a simple situation. The height from which he jumps should be limited by his control in landing; if the landing surface is hard (a floor or sidewalk) it should be covered with a mat or rug. Tires of different sizes may be placed on the ground or floor for children to jump into and out of; ropes and boards may be used in similar fashion.

Small jumping standards should be provided for playground use so that children may practice jumping *up* and the children should be taught to use these so that the bar will fall to the side of the landing; if a bar or rope is held for jumping it should always be held loosely and allowed to fall if the jumper's foot hits it.

Strips of colored cloth or plastic may be graduated in length and hung above head height for jump and reach practice.

The bounce board is useful equipment for two, three, and four year olds and offers sufficient variety for five year olds if the board is strong enough. In kindergarten balloon tires may be covered with canvas and used in much the same way. These require greater control on the part of the children. A useful substitute for a bounce board is a set of bed springs covered with canvas.

9. *Slides and swings* Slides and swings are found on many playgrounds. They are useful for orientation to space and position, for learning about passive movement, levers, pendulums, gravity, and other aspects of mechanics; they are also useful but limited for motor development. The swings especially are very soothing for some troubled children; they require considerable space and their use must be supervised for the safety of the children using them and for the safety of others on the playground. These pieces of equipment should be located away from other play centers and height limits should be in keeping with the age and size of the children.

List of Useful Equipment

Equipment must be available in needed quantity and it must be varied according to children's needs. The following items are suggested:

Balance boards—for construction details see Appendix p. 111.

Balls—of various sizes and materials.

Barrels—for creeping through, for rolling in, and for imaginative play.

Bars—firmly fixed and at varied heights for hanging, swinging, turning.

Bats—paddles, mallets.

Batting tees—these should be adjustable; they may be made of galvanized pipe and pieces of old garden hose.

Bean bags.

Benches—these must be sturdy but light enough for children to carry; they can be used for jumping, as inclined planes, and for vaulting.

Blocks, bricks, stones, and boards—for building and for carrying, lifting, pushing, and pulling.

Boards—these should be well-cured, smooth and 6 to 8 inches wide; cleats underneath or hooks on the ends allow various attachments.

Bounce board—this may be purchased or constructed.
See Appendix, p. 110.

Boxes—sturdy wooden boxes and large corrugated cardboard boxes such as those refrigerators come in.

Space, Time, and Equipment 93

Cargo nets (climbing nets)—these may be obtained as Army-Navy surplus or from regular supply sources; they are useful for a variety of climbing activities.

Climbing structures—sturdy arrangements of metal tubing sometimes called towers, jungle gyms, etc. The larger ones are permanent fixtures; smaller structures are portable but also must be very sturdy.

Flip-It Bowling Set—a useful device easily cared for; it may be purchased or constructed.

Hoops—for excellent suggestions for the use of these see L. Diem, (pp. 28-29) in References at end of this chapter.

Jumping standards—these may be easily constructed and are now commercially available in suitable sizes.

Ladders—to be used vertically, horizontally, and inclined at various angles; hooks on the end provide stable fixation.

Logs—short and long; poles with smooth surfaces.

Mats—small and washable for individual use; larger mats for small group activities; pads of foam rubber may be used temporarily.

Obstacle course—a wide variety of materials may be used to involve jumping, running, climbing, going over, under, and through.

Old bathtub—when appropriately set up is fine for water play.

Padded sawhorses, tables, and benches—may be used for vaulting and many tumbling activities instead of more expensive apparatus.

Parachute—may be obtained as Army-Navy surplus; see E. Hobson, (Chap. 7, pp. 31-33) in References at end of this chapter for ways of using.

Pitchback net—may be purchased or constructed; enables one child to play throw and catch.

Pool—portable plastic pool for wading and shallow water play.

Portable metal stands—these are light enough for children to carry but well constructed; they may be utilized with boards and ladders to make ever-changing apparatus.

Reach and jump target—strips of plastic graduated in length and suspended from a bar so that children may jump and reach to touch them.

Record player and records—readily available from many sources. Records selected should allow for creativity in movement.

Rhythm instruments—a sturdy drum is a must and should be used often by the teacher; rattles, drums, triangles, and many other instruments may be purchased or constructed.

Roller skates—these are not usual in nursery schools but may be used if facilities and space permit.

Rope ladder—one or more of these offer an interesting challenge and they are easily stored.

Ropes—long ropes are useful for turning and as climbing equipment; they may be used on the ground to mark off areas to jump over, to define floor patterns, etc. Short ropes for individual use may be used in countless ways. See Hobson, (Chap. 7, pp. 18-20) in References at end of this chapter.

Rugs—for outdoor use a blanket or sheet of foam rubber may be used as a rug. Small woven rugs may be used as substitutes for mats.

Slides and swings—these should be selected, located, and erected with professional advice.

Spades, rakes, shovels—these are available in small sizes and should be of strong construction.

Spools—large wooden spools are often discarded after utility construction; they should be weatherproofed and used for jumping, climbing, and building. They may also be rolled about the area.

Stairways—five to seven steps should be provided for a realistic experience. Many children do not use stairways at home or at school.

Stall bars—ladder-like bars erected close to a wall; these take up little space and are excellent for indoor use.

Suspended balls—good for hitting practice; require adequate space; should be pulled up after use.

Stools and tables—if strongly constructed these may be used for many purposes and old ones may be substituted for more expensive equipment.

Swedish vaulting box—available by purchase or construction, a very adaptable piece of equipment.

Swinging bridge—made of rope and boards and suspended about head height.

Targets—fixed or portable; these may vary widely in type—an open frame, concentric circles painted on cloth or plastic, flags or traffic cones for markers, and many others.

Tires—bicycle, car, and truck; tubes and casings. For suggestions in the use of these see Hobson (Chap. 1, p. 1) in References at end of this chapter.

Traffic cones—these may be available without cost or can be easily constructed. They are useful as markers and goals and may also be used as supports for light objects.

Tree trunks and stumps—wonderful for climbing, vaulting, jumping; they may be used as or converted into ships, horses, trucks, houses, etc.

Trestles and sawbenches—these may be used as supports for boards, ladders, and bridges. When constructed of wood the tops can be padded and used for vaulting and tumbling.

Tricycles and bicycles.

Tunnels—fabric and collapsible, concrete or ceramic.

Wagons, sleds, and wheelbarrows.

Walking beam—for construction see Appendix, p. 110.

Wands—smooth wooden sticks, also may be made of metal; the wooden ones are strong and inexpensive.

References

American National Red Cross. *Teaching Johnny to Swim.* Washington, D.C., 1957.

British Ministry of Education and Central Office of Information. *Moving and Growing* and *Planning the Programme.* Physical Education in the Primary School, Parts I (1952) and II (1953). London: Her Majesty's Printing Office, 1952-1953.

Diem, Liselott. *Who Can.* Frankfort, Germany: Wilhelm Limpert, 1967. (Available from Box 292, Trumbull, Connecticut.)

Friedberg, M. Paul. *Playgrounds for City Children.* Washington, D.C.: Association for Childhood Education, International, 1971.

Herkowitz, Jacqueline. "A Perceptual Motor Training Program to Improve the Gross Motor Abilities of Pre-Schoolers." *Journal of Health, Physical Education and Recreation* (April 1970): 30-47.

Hobson, Eve. *A Perceptual Motor Handbook and Guide to Its Planned Activities.* Operation Uplift, Title III, Richmond, Va.: Richmond Public Schools, 1971.

McCord, Ivalee H. "A Creative Playground." *Young Children* 26, no. 6 (August 1971): 342-47.

National Association for the Education of Young Children. *Play and Playgrounds.* Washington, D.C. (1834 Connecticut Ave., N.W.), 1970.

chapter eight

THE MOVEMENT PROGRAM

A program which features and enhances movement development is an educational program and as such should be conducted so as to contribute as much as possible to the child's total development. It is the educational discipline usually called physical education. Unfortunately physical education has, until recently, dealt with the school-age population only. It is probable that the first few years of life are the most significant for physical education. Physical education *is* movement education; it seeks to help people move well and for a great variety of purposes and it also has as a major goal contributing to all educational objectives—intellectual, social, physical, and emotional—through the medium of movement.

Ours is a sports-loving, movement-oriented culture, but far too little attention has been paid to the values of movement for young children. As our society becomes more urban, more industrial, more technological in its way of life, and as young children become more and more affected by these changes, parents and teachers must cooperate to provide adequately for the movement education of children during the early years.

THE PARENT-TEACHER RELATIONSHIP

The transfer of child from home to school is a severe challenge to the child's ability to adjust. It can be made easier for him if he visits the school in advance, if some of his playmates are also enrolled, if his mother visits with him, if he has an opportunity to become acquainted with his teacher in advance, and if he begins his enrollment with short sessions. Sometimes it helps to take a much loved toy for the first day or two. If the parent and teacher visit together for a few minutes each day the child is helped in his transition from home to school. The parent should understand that vigorous physical activity is part of the school day and that it is planned and conducted for educational purposes. The parent should be encouraged to observe this part of the program and his child's participation in it. Parent and teacher should share their interest in the child and discuss their observations and concerns.

The Home and the School

For some children the move from home to school is a complete change of environment. For one child it may be his first experience in sharing space with a group of other people; for another child it may be a venture into greater privacy—a cot of his own, a cubicle for *his* things, sufficient space to move about freely. Some children will be overwhelmed by so many books, so many blocks, crayons, and other materials which demand to be used; some will be frightened by the unfamiliar situation or frustrated because they had to leave their favorite toys at home.

A new enrollee should be given a tour of the area, introduced to new friends, and allowed to experiment briefly with unfamiliar equipment. If practicable he should be encouraged to try familiar activities in this new situation rather than be launched immediately into new skills and interests. Thereafter he should be encouraged to take a little of school home and to bring a little of home to school. If he has painted a picture or molded a rabbit he may wish to take it home; if he has learned to skip or to do a forward roll he should be encouraged to show his parents his new accomplishment; there should be "show and tell" opportunities both at home and at school. A young child takes great pride in his physical accomplishments. During the preschool years these constitute a vital resource for positive self-image; further enhancement comes from seeing his successes in the eyes of his parents.

Sharing Information

The child's medical record should be on file at the school or center. This record may be the result of a preentrance examination sponsored by the school or it may be a form supplied by the school and filled in by the child's pediatrician or family physician. It should be studied carefully by the teacher, referred to as needed, and kept up to date with notations by the school nurse or by the teacher. The parents should inform the teacher as health problems occur; the teacher must be alert to the child's reactions and when an injury, cold symptoms, or other health problems are observed the parent should be notified promptly.

In the same way teachers and parents should exchange information about all aspects of the child's development, including his progress in movement. Parents should be encouraged to play actively with their children and to share with them walks, snow play, visits to the beach, and outdoor games for mutual enjoyment. Teachers and parents should be aware of the physical development of the children; they should observe posture, strength, and alignment of the feet and legs, symmetry of the two sides of the body, rhythm and flow in movement. Their observations as to progress of all kinds—or lack of it—should be shared informally in notes and conferences. More formal exchange may take place in accordance with the policies of the school.

Sharing Responsibility

Parents, in the eyes of the law and society, are responsible for their children. They share this responsibility with others when a child, at a tender age, goes to nursery school for a morning or is placed in the custody of a day care center for the parents' working day. It is the parents' responsibility to make a good selection of a school or center, to take their child there and pick him up, to maintain a continuing contact with the personnel and program of the school, and to provide the best possible care and education at home. It is the school's or center's responsibility to be ready for the child each day, to provide the best care and education during the assigned portion of the day, and to stay with him and care for him until delivered to his parents. A well-coordinated program is essential. Teacher and parents should be working toward the same ends; the home should supplement the program of the school and vice versa. The child who gets a long afternoon nap at school may stay up a little longer and enjoy his parents' company at night; if outdoor time is limited at school (and unfortunately it may be!) there should be a long period in the yard or park when the child gets home. If the nursery school or kindergarten has limited play areas frequent weekend excursions to the park or open country are in order.

Appraisal and Referral

Teachers, and all parents are teachers too, must constantly appraise the progress which the children are making. For this purpose their best tools are awareness and observation. The first six chapters of this book are offered as aids in sharpening these tools—to help teachers to become more aware of how children move and to assist them in becoming more astute observers. Teachers and parents will share their observations and help each other in the solution of problems but sometimes other help must be sought also. When referrals are necessary they should be made in accordance with school policy, through the proper channels, and either by the parents or with parental consent.

With reference to movement development referrals may be necessary:

1. When a child is observed to have a persistent and marked asymmetry in body structure—the head deviates to one side, one hip is more prominent than the other, one shoulder is high, etc.
2. When a child appears to have a structural limitation or abnormality—the spinal column deviates left or right, the shoulder blades are prominent and the chest flat, the arches of the feet disappear when standing, the child is misshapen in any way.
3. When a child has a marked and persistent asymmetry in movement—when one limb or joint is more restricted than that on the opposite side of the body, when the child walks or runs with a limp or unevenly.
4. When a child exhibits marked tension in or distortion of his movements over a protracted period. These may be symptomatic of emotional disturbance or they may be of other origin; they should be studied in relation to the total behavior of the child.
5. If the child fails to show progressive development in his ability to move easily and with increasing strength, speed, and efficiency. Improvement by spurts rather than by steady progress is to be expected and is not a cause for grave concern; occasional retrogression is also quite normal, but some progress is normal expectancy if not from day to day then certainly from week to week and month to month.
6. If a child lags behind children of similar age in several (at least four or five) movement tasks and this lag persists for several months.

If a referral is contemplated because of one or more of the conditions described, the problem should first be considered in relation to all aspects of the child's behavior and progress. Some other solution for the problem may be found or if a referral is made, more complete information can be supplied.

ASSESSING THE PROGRAM

J.B. Nash, an eminent educator, wrote, "Joy is a sign that growth and development are proceeding harmoniously."[1] If the child is happy at school, if he goes cheerfully to school every day, if he comes home exuberant and full of his accomplishments, if he sleeps and eats well—the indications are that the school is doing a good job, the program is a good one, and the child's education is proceeding satisfactorily.

It is not always this way, of course; children have good and bad days; some children are not happy and some do not let their happiness shine forth. However, children are wonderfully adaptable and some can be happy with very little. Happiness is only one criterion but a very significant one for assessing the program.

Challenge is an essential ingredient of a good program. It is the greatest motivating force available. Challenge is present in a situation which provides evenly (or almost evenly) balanced chances of success and failure. Novelty offers challenge because it must be tried to see if it can be done! Once tried there will be more trials either for the satisfaction of success or for the feeling of growing achievement. Novelty is the spur to a young child that competition offers in later childhood and adulthood. But even for young children very easy tasks soon lose their charm and new elements or more difficult adaptations must be sought. For older children and especially the kindergarteners some creative movement in groups, simple games, song plays, and dance is recommended.

For *all* children novelty in itself is a stimulus and both the playground and the classroom should be changed from day to day so that a new arrangement may bring new ideas and new or unfamiliar equipment may enhance creativity and learning. A nursery school teacher may find endless variations in utilizing four lightweight but sturdy trestles and ten or twelve six-inch boards (smooth and sealed against the weather). Within a structure built of these a child may climb, creep, slide, balance, jump, and do many other movements. He can create his own sequence and repeat it over and over; he may imitate another child or work with him; he may practice one skill; the teacher may set a task or series of tasks for the child; or, under supervision, a child or several children may set tasks for others as in Follow the Leader.

Security is an essential of a good program. Security is offered by the familiar, the known, the well-loved aspects of the program. Comfort contributes to security—warmth, appetizing food, pleasant sounds, good lighting. Security is offered and confidence is supplied by move-

---

[1]Jay B. Nash, *Physical Education: Interpretations and Objectives* (New York: A.S. Barnes and Company, 1948), p. 22.

ment tasks and activities which the child knows he can do; security is also enhanced by rhythmic movement, especially repetitive movements in slow tempo such as swinging, swaying, and some forms of dance. It is often good to do the things we know we can do.

Good program requires effort. The heart and skeletal muscles of the body grow stronger from use at near-maximum effort. Children should be encouraged to exert their strength, to run as fast as possible, to throw as far as they can. But it is important not to set arbitrary standards and not to have the child experience repeated frustration.

Of course, the best indication of successful program is the steady development and progress of the children in the program.

THE MOVEMENT PROGRAM AT HOME

The home environment may be quite adequate for the movement development of the young child. In the country or a small town space is usually available. For the urban dweller, and certainly for one who lives in an apartment, providing space may be more difficult. Modern housing developments provide play areas and in some cities neighborhood parks are prevalent—factors which should be considered when the home site is chosen. Such areas require attendance and supervision by the parent unless a satisfactory arrangement for shared responsibility can be worked out. Even so the parents should take an active part in the movement experience of the young children—see that the playground is clean and well equipped, play with their children often, take them on outdoor excursions, and provide facilities for active play indoors.

If the home has its own outdoor play space it should be fenced, well turfed and provided with some of the equipment listed in chapter seven. It is likely to become a neighborhood center so parents must decide how, when, and by whom it may be used. Its use by neighborhood children should not be permitted beyond the limits of supervision provided, since ownership entails responsibility, legal and otherwise.

For indoor play which is not too restricted the child needs a place of his own—his own or a shared room, an alcove of the kitchen, service room or living room. In these areas Mother can help and offer companionship and supervision while she works; certainly one or both parents should schedule some time each day to participate with the child (or children). Attics and basements often provide spacious areas but may be so remote that they can be used only when a parent or older sibling can be there with the small children.

For indoor areas a well-padded, durable rug is invaluable; thus equipped the living room may be used for floor play on occasions. There should be a minimum of breakable objects in the play area; plastic, cloth, and yarn balls will be useful though other balls may have to be restricted to outdoor use; horizontal and vertical ladders near the wall conserve space, and stall bars against the wall may be used similarly. Other equipment suggested for schools and centers may be adapted for the home. Used household equipment can be retired or converted for the child at home since it will not get the hard wear of school equipment. All safety precautions must be observed—doors must be removed from refrigerators, trunks, old wardrobes, etc.; boards, ladders, and wood furniture must be strong and free from splinters.

HELPING CHILDREN LEARN

1. All young children are motivated by watching other children and are usually anxious to try the motor tasks they see other children do. They are content to imitate or emulate rather than compete. And they learn by imitation.

2. If a young child watches other children as they perform some movement feat with evident interest but does not try it himself, do not urge him; he is acquiring "know-how" and "readiness." He may be invited to try, or if he is especially shy or timid he might be encouraged and helped after an appropriate interval.

3. When a young child indicates unwillingness to attempt a new movement task his wishes should usually be respected. Children are remarkably fine judges of their own abilities; children are safer when they are operating within their own estimates of proficiency. Sometimes the child may substitute a different task which he knows he can do (he may gallop instead of skipping); sometimes the task may be adjusted within his limits (the bar on the jumping standard may be lowered); sometimes he may watch the other children thus learning from them; sometimes it helps just to wait a few days—or even weeks.

4. All children will not reach the same level of performance. If Johnny seems to be trying, accept his best efforts as "good" for Johnny and do not urge him to run faster or climb higher because some other child did. Interest in competition will come later when Johnny is more able to cope with it and when it will be more fruitful as a motivator.

5. Unless urged by adults or older children young children are seldom interested in competition; they are interested in what *they* can do, not in the accomplishments of others. A few children seek competition at ages five and six; when they do it should be recognized and carefully directed since it may develop into either a constructive drive or one that

is destructive. A child who learns early to be comfortable with competition is well armored for many of life's ordeals. He should enjoy victory without undue preening and experience defeat undismayed. He should learn early that competition and cooperation are two sides of the same coin and that there is both a top and a bottom.

6. Unless urged by adults or older children little ones will seldom exert themselves beyond their need for rest. They will play vigorously for a while and then go to the sand pile or find some other quiet activity. But since the planned environment and the presence of other children are in themselves very stimulating, teachers must plan for alternating periods of activity and rest, for vigorous movement and quiet play. And they must be ever alert for signs of fatigue especially among the children who have been recently ill.

7. Children under seven are seldom interested in the intangibles of motor performance. Scores and measures such as those of height, distance, time, the number of successful tries, etc., have little meaning for them. The *doing* is most important; the child wants to be seen doing it; he wants to be recognized as having done it. The younger child relies chiefly upon the approval of his parents and teachers—the adults of his world. At ages four and five children are beginning to be more aware of the approval of their peers though adult approval is still very important to them.

Teachers will wish to keep some records and those of time and distance are useful from four years of age on, even though they may be found to vary greatly.

8. Too often outdoor play areas are the same day after day. Teachers should plan for some variation of equipment and its use daily. On a weekly or monthly basis new centers may be constructed or the whole area may be rearranged.

For daily variation a few new boards, a tarp to serve as a shelter, a few lengths of tree trunk smoothly cut, several mats placed end to end—any one of these will arouse the children's interest; the teacher may help them to find ways of using the new equipment.

9. Boys seem to seek more vigorous movement than girls and for longer periods of time. The program should allow for this. Among the indoor centers girls tend to use the housekeeping and doll centers more than boys; boys will use the active play center (climbers, beams, tumbling mats) more than girls and probably the carpentry center also. No doubt both social mores and biological drives are causal factors. Too long schools have neglected or suppressed the young child's—and particularly the male child's—need for physical activity.

10. Motivation is no problem in the movement education of young children. They *want* to move; experience is a great teacher, and trial and error is an effective, though not infallible, way of learning. The teacher must be expert in knowing how and when to help the child. Sometimes to hold his hand is enough; this lends confidence and support. Sometimes the teacher must do some intensive study or seek other professional help before he can intervene. The teacher too will find trial and error and experience great assets.

11. Proper goal setting is important in helping children to achieve. In movement education as in other areas of learning, goals must be selected which are meaningful to the child and which he can grasp. His vocabulary is small—so the goals must be expressed briefly and in simple words. The target should be tangible and easily recognized, for example, "Run to me!" for the two year olds; "Run to the fence!" for three year olds; "Run across the line!" for the older children.

12. Language is a part of movement education. A child should learn the right names for the movements he uses and the games he plays. The four year old should recognize overhand and underhand throws; sliding and skipping; pushing and pulling, etc. Later, but probably not before age seven, he should be able to describe each movement. He should learn the names of the different pieces of equipment and be able to distinguish between them as to shape, size, material, and use.

13. Small children are very possessive and naturally so. It is not wrong for them to be self-centered; it is just wrong for them to stay that way! They learn by sharing, by trading interests and toys, by taking turns. They also learn by disputing and contending; if allowed they will usually work out a settlement. The wise teacher will not intervene too quickly and when he does will help the disputers to an agreement if possible.

14. Even though early childhood is a period of vigorous activity young children tend to start, stop, and make changes slowly. Do not hurry them; some time to "dawdle" (it seems like dawdling to the adult) is essential for perception and for learning. The world is a new and interesting place; there is much to arouse—and distract—the little one's awareness.

15. Older children should sometimes play with younger children. Older children are great teachers and can help the younger ones. Younger children are great imitators—they will learn much by imitation but they will also get new ideas, make new friends, reach another notch or two upward.

16. It is difficult for an adult to conceive of past experience of so short a duration as two years. To a child of two or even three "to have done it"—to have had an experience *just one time* is comparable to that of an adult who has, perhaps, had a short course in a subject. And the impact of the experience on the child's ego, and within his stimulus-response system and his memory storehouse is tremendous and much greater than if it occurs in later life. Months later a small child will know that he once climbed that ladder (or jumped off that bench, or rolled over the sawbuck); he remembers that he did it and he remembers *how*. He will approach the task with the confidence of an old hand.

17. The child's drive for movement is a ready lever to the teacher's hand. Because the children *want* to move, active play becomes a medium through which children readily learn politeness, sharing, consideration, and other desirable social traits. Later on, and particularly in games, the child's joyful participation offers experience in moral judgments—what is fair, what is allowed by the rules, how to compromise without sacrificing principle—and even though his interests are self-centered he will sublimate them in order to participate.

18. It is almost always unwise to impose a pattern of movement upon the child. Let him instead find his own. If the time is ripe and his experiences have been adequate he will achieve a crude representation of the basic pattern within his first few attempts. If he does not, help him to practice simpler tasks, preferably those using some of the same elements, until a later date.

CURRICULUM

Curriculum construction should be the shared responsibility of teachers and administrators. Curricula are usually most satisfactory when constructed for a particular school system or a particular school. A few suggestions are offered here concerning the movement aspects (physical education) of the curriculum for young children:

1. Through age five, approximately one-half of the school day should be devoted to activity which is largely physical.
2. Though both gross and fine motor activities should be included, the younger the child the greater the emphasis should be on gross motor.
3. Though both boys and girls need much vigorous movement for best development, it is probable that boys will profit from movement of greater duration and intensity, and that for them close visual work and the more sedentary occupations should be deferred or kept to less than half of the total time.

4. The general characteristics of movement (the eight mentioned in chapter four and perhaps others) constitute a framework on which curriculum for young children can be built. These may be thought of as desirable objectives and also considered as outcomes by which the program can be appraised.
5. The movement tasks listed in chapter two, supplemented by others appropriate for a particular group, may be used as the elements or activities of which the program is constructed. They must be selected, arranged, varied, combined, and developed in a diversity of ways most appropriate for the purposes desired and the children to be served.
6. Physical education for young children is an integral part of the total curriculum and should permeate each day's program; it should reach into and grow out of the language, art, music, science, health, and other aspects of the program. Dance and music may be developed together. Active games and stories may be combined. Field excursions may result in new science and movement experiences. "Show and tell" sessions may display new learnings in language and in physical feats.
7. Equipment should be selected and used purposefully. The first question should be, "What may the children use this for?"
8. Long-term planning and day-to-day planning are both essential if educational goals are to be achieved in moving and through movement.

References

Akers, Milton. "Today with Young Children." *Virginia Conference on Movement Experiences for Young Children*. Edited by Eleanor Bobbitt. Farmville, Va.: Longwood College, 1971.

Barsch, Ray H. *A Perceptual Motor Curriculum*. Seattle, Washington: Special Child Publishing Co., 1967.

British Ministry of Education and Central Office of Information. *Moving and Growing* and *Planning the Program*, Parts I and II. *Physical Education in the Primary School*. London: Her Majesty's Stationery Office, 1952-1953.

Butler, Annie. *Current Research in Early Childhood Education*. Washington, D.C.: American Association of Elementary-Kindergarten-Nursery Education, 1970, pp. 78-106, 126-32.

Dance Task Force, AAHPER. Gladys Fleming, Chairman. "Report" (June 1971, 13-22) and "Over the Country Children Are Dancing," *Journal of Health, Physical Education and Recreation* 42, no.'s 6 and 8 (October 1971): 27-34.

Halverson, Lolas E. "A Real Look at the Young Child." *Journal of Health, Physical Education and Recreation* 42, no. 5 (May 1971): 31-33.

Howard, Shirley. "The Movement Education Approach to Teaching in English Elementary School." *Trends in Elementary School Physical Education,* pp. 14-16, Washington, D.C.: American Association for Health, Physical Education and Recreation, 1970.

Jones, Alma Ward. "Now and Tomorrow." *Virginia Conference on Movement Experiences for Young Children.* Edited by Eleanor Bobbitt. Farmville, Va.: Longwood College, 1971.

Porter, Lorena. *Movement Education for Children.* Washington, D.C.: American Association for Elementary-Kindergarten-Nursery Educators, 1969.

Russell, Joan. *Creative Dance in the Primary School.* London: Macdonald and Evans, 1965.

APPENDIX

Details of Figure-8-Run

A central starting point is marked in red; four blocks are placed at distances of 20 feet to mark a square of which the corners are equal distances from the central point. Starting at the center the child is instructed to run around the opposite blocks in two figure 8's, always returning to the center (red-1-red-2-red-3-red-4-red).

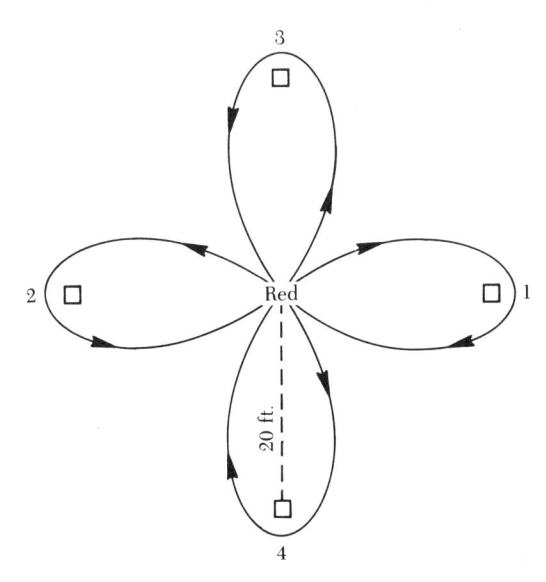

Construction of Bounce Board

1. Select a piece of ¾-inch marine plywood 2 by 8 feet, free from knots and other imperfections; weatherproof it with a good sealer.
2. Fasten cleats (2 by 2 by 18 inches) 2 inches from each end with nails or screws; fasten a 4-inch length 2 by 2 inches at right angles to each end of each cleat to form a corner into which the top of the sawbuck will fit.
3. Construct two sturdy miniature sawbucks each 11 inches in height and 18 inches long.
4. Place the plywood over the sawbucks with the cleats against the tops; the cleats will keep the board from slipping.

Details of Bench Used for Pushing and Pulling

The bench should be sturdily constructed and smoothly finished. The top should measure 11 by 32 inches; it should be 16½ inches high. Nylon pads can be fastened to the four legs (rollers should not be used; the pads are available in most hardware stores and are fastened to chairs, table legs, etc., to provide easy gliding without scratching the floor).

The children enjoy "riding" this bench and being pushed or pulled by the other children.

Construction of Walking Beam

1. Select a piece of lumber 2 inches by 4 inches by 8 feet, dressed. Smooth and seal it.
2. Build brackets for the beam by cutting one piece 2 by 4 inch by 18 inches long, two pieces 8 inches long, and two pieces 7 inches long; nail or screw together to make two brackets as pictured. The beam may be supported with either the narrow or broad side up.

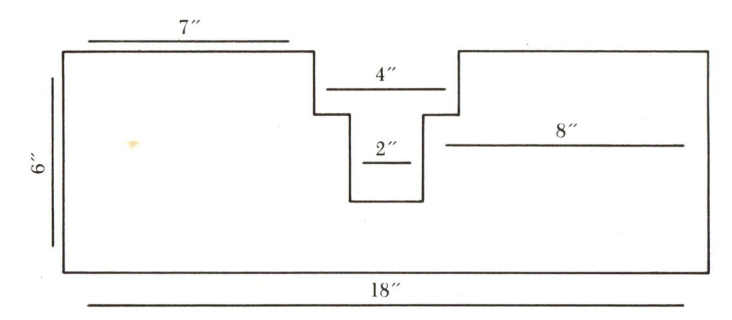

3. Place the beam in the brackets; the 4-inch side is useful until the child is about five years of age when the 2-inch side can be used for walking and other simple tasks.

Construction of Balance Board

1. Select an 18-inch square of ¾-inch plyboard and seal or finish it as desired.
2. Cut three bases 4 by 4 by 4 inches, 3 by 3 by 4 inches, and 2 by 2 by 4 inches. The bases may be changed to make balancing easier or more difficult.
3. Fasten a base to the board with a ⅜-inch bolt with wing nut. Counter sink bolt head to provide smooth bottom surface.

GLOSSARY

Active Movement   Movement in which all of the effort required is provided by muscular contraction of the person moving.

Agility   Maneuverability of the body; the ability to change the direction of the body or of parts of the body quickly and easily.

Ambidexterity   Ability to use both hands equally well.

Assistive Movement   Movement of a body part in which the person moving is assisted by another person or force but provides some of the effort himself.

Batting Tee   A small flexible stand from which a ball may be hit, usually adjustable for height.

Body Rotation   Axial or spiral movement of trunk or of body from foot to shoulders as in batting or throwing.

Bounce Board   A flexible board supported at either end and used by small children in trampoline fashion.

Broad Jump   A jump to cover distance, also termed a long jump. It may be preceded by a run in which case the takeoff is from one foot; when taken from a stand the takeoff is from both feet.

Cross (X) Lateral   An adjective applicable to movement in which opposite hand and foot are moved together.

114   Movement of the Young Child: Ages Two to Six

Developmental Age   Age based on maturity rather than years. Developmental quotient (DQ) is the child's maturity score adjusted for chronological age.

Dominance   Side preference for paired parts.

Dominant Foot   In this study the foot preferred for kicking.

Dominant Hand   In this study the hand preferred for throwing.

Dynamic Balance   Balance while moving (as opposed to static balance—like standing on one foot).

Dyslexia   Visual confusion by which similarly shaped letters cause the victim to transpose letters in reading.

Early Childhood   In this study the period following infancy and preceding the first grade of school; sometimes defined as ages two through eight but not so used in this book.

Eye-hand Efficiency   Effectiveness in manual response to a static or moving object.

Figure-8-run   A task requiring one to run in a figure-8 pattern; for details as used in this study see Appendix, p. 109.

Follow the Leader   A familiar game in which the leader sets a variety of movements and the other participants follow him in the movements.

Follow Through   In movement, that action which follows the climax of the task and in which built-up momentum is continued until decelerated or checked for balance and safety.

Galloping   In human movement, a two-part movement of uneven rhythm in which one foot leads, stepping forward; the other takes a shorter, following step; the movement is spritely and staccato.

Golgi Tendon Organs   Sensory receptor organs in tendons; they are stimulated by tension of the tendon either in contraction or stretching and are concerned chiefly with reflexes.

Homolateral Movement   Movement of two parts on the same side as right hand and right foot.

Joint Receptors   Sensory endings which are in the connective tissue in and around joints; they record the joint position and movement at the joint and are also concerned with reflexes.

Jumping   A movement through space from one foot to the same foot (as an elevated hop) or both feet; also a movement through space from both feet to one or both feet. Often used loosely to include a leap.

Kinesthesis   The sense of movement and position, including tension, direction, speed, etc.

Laterality   Awareness of sidedness within oneself and with reference to oneself; awareness of right and left.

Leap   A movement through space from one foot to the other; an elevated running step.

Mental Age Age based on mental ability rather than years. Intelligence quotient (IQ) represents the child's intelligence (mental ability) score adjusted for chronological age.

Mixed Dominance Dominance in which at least one part preference is different from the others; as right-handed, right-eyed, and left-footed.

Motor Planning A type of planning in which two or more motor elements or acts are involved and in which the person planning must foresee his actions in a sequence.

Motor Score For this study, the total of all motor task scores for a given age adjusted for the number of tasks included (so that all motor scores are comparable at all ages).

Motor Task Score In this study a score derived by assigning two points for success, an additional point for basic pattern, a fourth point for additional elements of the task, and a fifth point for demonstrating all elements listed.

Movement Education Education which seeks to educate in movement and through movement; in this study synonomous with physical education. Sometimes (but not in this book) used as synonomous with movement exploration.

Movement Exploration In education, the use of familiar ways of moving in order to find new ways, new uses and new meanings, sometimes (but not in this book) used as synonomous with movement education.

Muscle Spindle A receptor organ which is found in most muscles; each consists of tiny muscle fibers and both motor and sensory nerve fibers. It responds to both stretch and contraction of the muscle and probably helps to monitor all movement.

Negative Findings A medical term meaning no abnormalities found on examination.

Opposition In movement, the use of opposite hand and foot as in walking (left foot and right hand move forward together) and throwing (weight is shifted to the left foot as right hand moves forward for throw).

Passive Movement Movement in which no effort is supplied by the person moving; gravity is often the supplying force (as when a person drops from a hanging position to the ground); in physical therapy passive movement is often used.

Physical Education That discipline which seeks to improve the individual's movement and to educate through the medium of movement.

Pike One of three recognized body positions in gymnastics (the others are tuck and straight); in a pike the legs are straight and the hands and torso approach or touch the legs and feet; sometimes called a jackknife.

Poor Pussy A simple game in which one person simulates a cat while another pats him on the head saying, "Poor Pussy."

Positive Findings Those findings of a medical examination which denote disease or abnormality.

Power   Used in this study to mean explosive force; strength exerted with great speed.

Proprioceptors   Those sensory or receptor organs which are within the body—are not superficial and have no external orifice.

Quadripedal   Meaning four-footed or moving on four parts (hands and feet or knees).

Referral   Used in education to mean referred to a special officer or outside agency for expert help or consultation.

Rhythmic Pattern   The pattern of rhythm built by varying the time intervals between sounds or accents; each pattern may have one or more parts before repetition; the walk is one-part and even; the skip is two-part and uneven; the waltz is three-part and even; etc.

Sliding   In locomotion a two-part movement of uneven rhythm in which, with body facing forward, the right (or left) foot steps sideward repeatedly; the other foot closes to the leading foot with a shorter, quicker step.

Step Pattern   A combination of steps which is usually repeated; the skip repeats a hop-step, first on one foot then on the other; in sliding a child repeats a long and then a short step, always to the same side unless there is a change of direction.

Total Body Assembly   The condition of using the parts of the body in harmony according to the requirements of the movement in achieving its purpose—especially for achieving force, speed, or power, or a combination of these.

Transfer of Weight   The transfer of weight from one foot to the other; more specifically a transfer backward in preparation and forward in delivering and follow through—as in throwing.

Tuck   One of three recognized body positions in gymnastics (the others are pike and straight); in the tuck the body is drawn into a ball with neck, trunk, and legs flexed.

X-Lateral   See Cross Lateral.

BIBLIOGRAPHY

American Association for Health, Physical Education and Recreation. *Approach to Perceptual Motor Programs*. Washington, D.C.: 1970. Also in *Journal of Health and Physical Education* (April 1970): 30-47.

—————. *Challenge*. Published five times each school year, Washington, D.C. (1201 16th St., N.W.).

—————. *Perceptual Motor Foundations: A Multidisciplinary Concern*. Proceedings of the Perceptual Motor Symposium, Washington, D.C.: 1969.

American National Red Cross. *Teaching Johnny to Swim*. ARC 1096, Washington, D.C.: American National Red Cross, 1957.

Andrews, Gladys. *Creative Rhythmic Movement for Children*. New York: The Macmillan Company, 1958.

Apell, R.J., and R.W. Lawry, Jr. *Preschool Vision*. 4030 St. Louis, Mo.: American Optometric Association (4030 Chouteau Ave.), 1959.

Arbuckle, Wanda Rector; Eleanor Hill Ball; and George L. Cornwell. *Learning to Move and Moving to Learn*. Book II: *Animals*. Columbus, Ohio; Charles E. Merrill Publishing Co., 1973.

Arlington County Public Schools. *Movement Experiences for Elementary Children, Kindergarten, Grades 1-2*. Arlington, Va.: 1969.

Association for Childhood Education International. *Physical Education for Children's Healthful Living*. Washington, D.C.: 1968.

Barsch, Roy H. *A Perceptual Motor Curriculum.* Seattle, Washington: Special Child Publishing Co., 1967.

──────. "Perceptual Motor Efficiency." In *Perceptual Motor Curriculum,* vol. 1. Seattle, Washington: Special Child Publications, Seattle Seguin School, 1967.

Bayley, Nancy. "The Development of Motor Abilities During the First Three Years," *Monograph of the Society for Research in Child Development* 1(1935): 1-26. Washington, D.C. (Available from 16 E. 46th St., New York, N.Y. 10017: Kraus Reprint Corporation.)

Bloom, Benjamin S. *Early Learning in the Home.* ERIC No. EDO19 127. Los Angeles: University of California, 1965.

──────. *Stability and Change in Human Characteristics.* New York: John Wiley and Sons, 1964.

Braley, William T.; Geraldine Konicki; and Catherine Leedy. *Daily Sensori Motor Training Activities.* Freeport, N.Y.: Educational Activities, Inc., 1968.

Butler, Annie. *Current Research in Early Childhood Education.* Washington, D.C.: American Association of Elementary-Kindergarten-Nursery Educators, 1970.

Carr, Constance. *Music for Children's Living.* Washington, D.C.: Association for Childhood Education International, 1970.

Cherry, Clare. *Creative Movement for the Developing Child.* Palo Alto, Calif.: Fearon Publishers, 1968.

Cooper, John M., and Ruth B. Glassow. *Kinesiology.* St. Louis: C.V. Mosby Company, 1963.

Cratty, Bryant J. *Active Learning.* Englewood Cliffs, N.J.: Prentice-Hall, Inc., 1971.

──────. *Developmental Sequences of Perceptual Motor Tasks.* Freeport L.I., New York: Educational Activities, Inc., 1967.

Cratty, Bryant J., and Sister Margaret Mary Martin. *Perceptual Motor Efficiency in Children.* Philadelphia: Lea and Febiger, 1969.

De Harb, Ellen. "What's Involved in Being Able to Read?" *Young Children* (March 1968): 202-10.

de Hirsch, Katrina; Jeanette Jefferson Jansky; and William B. Langford. *Predicting Reading Failure.* New York: Harper and Row, 1966.

Diem, Liselott. *Who Can.* Frankfort, Germany: Wilhelm Limpert, 1967. (Available Box 292, Trumbull, Connecticut.)

Dunsing, Jack D., and Newell C. Kephart. "Motor Generalizations in Space and Time." In *Learning Disorders.* Edited by Jerome Helmulke, vol 1, pp. 77-121. Seattle, Washington: Special Child Publications, 1965.

Espenschade, Anna S., and Helen M. Eckert. *Motor Development.* Columbus, Ohio: Charles E. Merrill Publishing Company, 1967.

Bibliography

Flavell, J.H. *The Developmental Psychology of Jean Piaget.* Princeton, N.J.: Van Nostrand Co., Inc., 1963.

Flinchum, Betty M., and Margie R. Hanson. "Who Says the Young Child Can't?" Journal of Health, Physical Education, and Recreation (June 1972): 16-19.

Frostig, Marianne with Phyllis Maslow. *Movement Education: Theory and Practice.* Chicago: Follett Educational Corporation, 1970.

Gardner, Bruce. *Development in Early Childhood.* New York: Harper & Row, 1964.

Gesell, Arnold L. *The First Five Years of Life.* New York: Harper & Row, 1940.

Getman, G.N. "The Visuo Motor Complex in the Acquisition of Learning Skills." In *Learning Disorders.* Edited by Jerome Helmulke, vol. 1. Seattle, Washington: Special Child Publication, Seattle Seguin School, Inc., 1965.

Gitter, Lena L. *The Montessori Way.* Seattle, Washington: Special Child Publications, 1970.

Glogau, Lillian, and Edmund Krause. *Let's See: An Educational Activity-Book Full of Fun for 5-7 Year Olds.* St. Louis: American Optometric Association, 1970.

Godfrey, Barbara B., and Newell C. Kephart. *Movement Patterns and Motor Education.* New York: Appleton-Century-Crofts, 1969.

Hackett, Layne C., and Robert Jenson. *A Guide to Movement Exploration.* Palo Alto, Calif.: Peek Publications, 1967.

Halverson, Lolas E. "Development of Motor Patterns in Young Children." *Quest* (May 1966): 44-53.

Harvat, Robert W. *Physical Education for Children with Perceptual-Motor Learning Disabilities.* Columbus, Ohio: Charles E. Merrill Publishing Co., 1971.

Herkowitz, Jacqueline. "A Perceptual Motor Training Program to Improve the Gross Motor Abilities of Pre-Schoolers." *Journal of Health, Physical Education, and Recreation* (April 1970): 35-47.

Hobson, Eve. *A Perceptual Motor Handbook and Guide to Its Planned Activities.* Operation Uplift, Title III, Richmond, Va.: Richmond Public Schools, 1971.

Hunt, Valerie. "Movement Behavior: A Model for Action." *Quest.* Monograph II (April 1964): 69-91.

Hymes, James L., Jr. *Early Childhood Education: An Introduction to the Profession.* Washington, D.C.: National Association for the Education of Young Children, 1968.

Ilg, Frances, and Louise Bates Ames, *Child Behavior.* New York: Harper & Row, 1955.

Ismail, A.H., and Joseph J. Gruber. *Integrated Development: Motor Aptitude and Intellectual Performance.* Columbus, Ohio: Charles E. Merrill Publishing Co., 1967.

Jordan, Diana. *Childhood and Movement.* Oxford: Basil, Blackwood & Mott, Ltd., 1966. (Available from Ling House, 10 Nottingham Place, London, W.I., England.)

Kephart, Newell C. *The Slow Learner in the Classroom.* 2nd ed. Columbus, Ohio: Charles E. Merrill Publishing Co., 1971.

Kirchner, Glenn, Jean Cunningham, and Eileen Warrell. *Introduction to Movement Education.* Dubuque, Iowa: W.M.C. Brown Co., 1970.

Kritchevsky, Sybil, and Elizabeth Prescott, with Lee Walling. *Planning Environments for Young Children: Physical Space.* Washington, D.C.: National Association for the Education of Young Children, 1969.

Landreth, Catherine. *Early Childhood.* 2nd ed. New York: Alfred A. Knopf, 1967.

Latchaw, Marjorie, and Glen Egstrom. *Human Movement.* Englewood Cliffs, N.J.: Prentice-Hall, 1969.

McGraw, Myrtle B. *The Neuromuscular Maturation of the Human Infant.* Reprint. New York: Hafner Publishing Company, 1963. (Originally published Columbia University Press, 1945.)

National Association for Community Development. *Early Childhood Development: Outlook for 1970.* Washington, D.C. (16th St. N.W.), 1970.

National Association for the Education of Young Children. *Play and Playgrounds.* Washington, D.C. (Connecticut Ave., N.W.), 1970.

———. *The Significance of the Young Child's Motor Development.* Washington, D.C., 1971.

Nunn, Riba R., and Charles R. Jones. *The Learning Pyramid: Potential Through Perception.* Columbus, Ohio: Charles E. Merrill Publishing Co., 1972.

Pines, Maya. *Revolution in Learning, The Years From Birth to Six.* New York: Harper & Row, Publishers, Inc., 1967.

Porter, Lorena. *Movement Education for Children.* Washington, D.C.: American Association for Elementary-Kindergarten-Nursery Educators, 1969.

Quill, Jeanne W. *Creating with Material for Work and Play.* Washington, D.C.: Association for Childhood Education International, 1971.

Radler, D.H., and Newell C. Kephart. *Success Through Play.* New York: Harper & Row, 1960.

Rarick, G. Lawrence. *Motor Development During Infancy and Childhood.* Madison, Wisconsin: University of Wisconsin, College Printing and Typing Co., 1961.

Rasmussen, Margaret. *Play—Childrens' Business.* Washington, D.C.: Association for Childhood Education, International, 1970.

Russell, Joan. *Creative Dance in the Primary School*. London, England: MacDonald & Evans, 1965.

Schurr, Evelyn L. *Movement Experiences for Children*. New York: Appleton-Century-Crofts, 1967.

Sheehy, Emma D. *Children Discover Music and Dance*. Early Childhood Education Series, ed. Kenneth D. Wann, Columbia University, N.Y.: Teacher's College Press, 1968.

Simpson, Dorothy M. *Learning to Learn*. Columbus, Ohio: Charles E. Merrill Publishing Co., 1968.

Sinclair, Caroline B. *Movement and Movement Patterns of Early Childhood*. Richmond, Va.: State Department of Education, 1971.

Singer, Robert N. *Motor Learning and Human Performance*. New York: Macmillan Co., 1968.

Smith, Hope M. "Motor Activity and Perceptual Development; Some Implications for Physical Education." *JOHPER*, 39, no. 2 (1968): 28-33.

Smith, Paul. *Neuromuscular Skills for Assisting Neurophysiological Maturation*. Seattle, Washington 98155: Shoreline School District (412 N.E. 158th & 20th Ave., N.E.) 1967.

Stecher, Miriam B. "Concept Learning Through Movement Improvisation: The Teacher's Role as Catalyst." *Young Children*, 25, no. 3 January 1970: 143-53.

Sunderlin, Sylvia. *Nursery School Portfolio*. Washington, D.C.: Association for Childhood Education International, 1970.

Virginia Conference on Movement Experiences for Young Children. Edited by Eleanor Bobbitt. Farmville, Va.: Longwood College, 1971.

Walters, C. Etta. "Contributions of Child Development to Physical Education." *Proceedings Southern Association for Physical Education of College Women*. Memphis, Tenn.: 1969.

Wickstrom, Ralph L. *Fundamental Motor Patterns*. Philadelphia: Lea & Febiger, 1970.

INDEX

Acceleration, 8
Achievement, 5
  judging of, 12, 99-100 (see also Appraisal)
  measuring, 50, 52
Age:
  of expectancy, 13
  related to developing movement, 53-55
Agility, 11, 42, 48
Akers, Milton, 107
American Association for Health, Physical Education, and Recreation, 107
American National Red Cross, 95
Appraisal, 42, 52, 99-100
Ascending stairs, 12
Assessing the program, 101-2
  challenge, 101
  effort, 102
  joy, 101
  novelty, 101
  progress of children, 102
  security, 101-2
Asymmetry, 100
Atrophy, 3

Balance, 8
  dynamic, 41, 44-45
Balance beam (see Walking beam)
Balance board, construction of, 111
Barnhart, Clarence L., 89
Barsch, Ray H., 107
Basic movement, 8
Basic movement patterns, 34
Basic patterns, 12-30, 35-39
  achieving, 39
  emergence of, 39
  guides for achieving, 39
Batting tees, 90
Bayley, Nancy, 2
Beam (see Walking beam)
Bench:
  construction of, 110
  use of, 23
Bounce board:
  construction of, 110
  and other like equipment, 91-92
  use of, 12-13
Bouncing:
  a large ball, 13-14
  on the bounce board, 12-13
Brain damage, 33, 34

123

124 Index

British Ministry of Education and
    Central Office of Information, 95, 107
Butler, Annie, 107

Carrying, 14-15
    likeness to pushing and pulling, 38
    persistence in, 38
    total body assembly in, 38
Case studies, 65-77
Case studies, questions for, 67, 69, 71,
    72, 73-74, 75, 76-77
Catching a ball, 15
Challenge, 8, 85, 101
Chaney, Clara M., 64
Characteristics, general, of movement,
    (see General characteristics
    of movement)
Climbing, a ladder, 16-17
Clothing, 83-84
    shoes, 84
Cohen, Alan A., 64
Cohen, Dorothy H., 77
Competition, 103-4
Cooper, John M., 32, 34
Communication, through movement, 2
Cratty, Bryant J., 10, 64
Creativity, 63-64
    in learning, 63-64
    in teaching, 63
Creeping, 17-18
Cross-lateral patterning, 34
Curriculum:
    in movement, 8, 11, 106-7
    in movement education, 106-7
    in physical education, 106-7
    suggestions for, 106-7

Decision making, 8, 64
Demand, in Law of Use, 3-4
Descending stairs, 18
Development sequence, 32
Dewey, John, theory of learning by
    doing, 5
Diem, Liselott, 95
Differences, genetic, 5
Differences in movement, 53-64
    related to age, 53-55
    related to intelligence, 58-59
    related to race, 58
    related to reading readiness, 59
    related to sex, 55-58
    related to teachers' estimates of
        achievement, 60
Distance throwing, 90
Dominance, 42, 49-50, (table), 51
Dunsing, Jack D., 32

Eckert, Helen S., 30
Efficiency, eye-hand, 42, 47-48
Efficiency, synaptic, 5
Effort, 102
Elements, of tasks, 12-30
Environment, 79
Environmental influences, 32
Equilibrium, 3
Equipment, 86-95
    for balance, 89
    for ball handling, 90
    for climbing, 88
    for creeping and other floor
        movement, 88
    criteria for, 86-87
    list of useful, 92-95
    for opposition, development of, 88-89
    purposeful use of, 87-92
    for resistance activities, 90-91
    for rhythms, development of, 89
    slides and swings, 92
Espenschade, Anne S., 30
Exercise:
    pacemaker for health, 2
    organic health, contribution to, 3
Exteroceptors, 3
Eye-hand coordination, 47
Eye-hand efficiency, 42, 47,
    (table), 48

Feedback:
    mechanism, 4, 5
    in movement, 3
    reenforcement, 35
    through sensory organs, 34
    through social reaction, 34
Figure-8-run, 11
    details of, 109
    directions for, 18-19
Flavell, J.H., 10
Fleming, Gladys, 107
Follow-through, 37
Force, total body assembly for, 41,
    (table), 46
Forward roll, 18
Four-part movements, 35
    climbing, 35
    creeping, 35
    swimming, 36
Friedberg, M. Paul, 95
Fundamental movements, 6, 8

Gallop, 19
    in rhythmic two-part locomotion, 46-47
    as related to the skip and slide, 36
Gardner, Elizabeth B., 4-5, 32

General characteristics of movement, 107
  agility, 42, 48
  dominance, 42, 49-50
  dynamic balance, 41, 44-45
  eye-hand efficiency, 42, 47-48
  opposition and symmetry, 41, 42-43
  postural adjustment, 42, 49
  rhythmic two-part locomotion, 42, 46-47
  total body assembly, 41, 45-46
General characteristics of movement, contribution of, 52
Genetic foundation, 7
Genetic influences, 32
Gesell, Arnold L., 1, 6
Gitter, Lena L., 10
Glassow, Ruth B., 2, 32, 34
Goal:
  meaningful, 34-35
  setting, 39, 105
  tangible, 35
Goals:
  in movement for young children, 8
  of movement education, 97
  of physical education, 97
Godfrey, Barbara B., 40
Golgi tendon organs, 3
Goodenough, F. L., 2
Gutteridge, Mary V., 2

Halverson, Lolas E., 32, 34, 40, 77, 107
Handicapped child, 2 (see also Brain damaged)
Hanging, 19-20
Health:
  exercise as a pacemaker for, 2
  good, 32
  organic, 3
Helping children:
  to independence, 62
  to learn, 103-6
Heredity, (see Genetic influences)
Heredity, and maturation, 6
Herkowitz, Jacqueline, 95
High jump, running, 24
Hitting, 20-21
Hobson, Eve, 95
Home:
  movement program at, 102-3
  and the school, 98
  sharing information with 98-99
Hopping, 7, 21-22, 36
Howard, Shirley, 108
Huelsman, Charles B., Jr., 52
Human nature, complexity of, 5
Human personality, diversity of, 5
Hunt, Valerie E., 52

Individual approach, to teaching, 60-63
Individual differences, 5-60
Input, 34, 77
Input system, 3
Intelligence, related to developing movement, 58-59
Interaction, 6, 33, 63
Interaction with the world around, 79

Joint receptors, 3
Jones, Alma Ward, 108
Judging achievement, 12, 98-99
Jump, 36
  from both feet, 7
  running high, 24
  standing broad, 26-27
  standing long, 91 (see also Standing broad)
Jumping, 91
Jumping standards, 91

Kephart, Newell C., 32, 40, 64
Kicking, 22
  as a form of striking, 38
Kinesthesis, 3

La Grange, Fernand, 4
Landing:
  control in, 37
  safety in, 37, 91
Laterality, 8
Law of Use, physiological, 2-4
Leap, 36
Learning:
  concommitant, 8
  from experiences, 5
  helping children with, 103-6
  through movement, 7, 9
  movement as an essential in, 10
Life span:
  period of, 31
  time system in, 6
Locomotion:
  movements of, 7
  rhythmic two-part, 42, 47

McCloy, Charles Harold, 42
McCord, Ivalee H., 95
McGraw, Myrtle B., 6, 32, 40
Martin, Sister Mary Margaret, 64
Mastery:
  of self, 2
  of environment, 2
Maturation, 6
  as heredity at work, 6
  influenced by learning, 31
  and learning, 6

Maturation, (Cont.)
  reenforced, 7
Meaning of movement, 9-10
Measuring achievement, 50, 52
Medical record, 98
Metheney, Eleanor, 10
Momentum, 8
Montessori, Maria, 5
Motor development:
  of infants, 1-2
Motor learning, 5
Motor planning, 11
Motor tasks, (see Movement tasks)
Movement:
  as education, 1
  as essential to learning, 10
  as a learning experience, 2
  meaning of, 9-10
  as a medium for learning, 7-8
  for movements sake, 11
  values of, 2
  what it means, 9-10
  in young child's world, 9
Movement education, 97
Movement patterns, 32, 33-40
  likenesss in, 7, 38, 41
  related movements in, 35-38
  sequence of, 6
  similarities in, 12-30, 53 (see also Likeness in)
Movement program:
  at home, 102-3
  for young children, 97-108
Movement tasks:
  details of, 11-30
  in longitudinal study, 6-7
  selected as fundamental, 11-30
    ascending stairs, 12
    bouncing on the bounce board, 12
    bouncing a large ball, 13
    carrying, 14
    catching a ball, 15
    climbing a ladder, 16
    creeping, 17
    descending stairs, 18
    figure-8-run, 18
    forward roll, 18
    galloping, 19
    hanging, 19-20
    hitting, 20-21
    hopping, 21-22
    kicking, 22
    pulling, 23
    pushing, 23
    running, 23-24
    running high jump, 24
    skipping, 24

Movement tasks, (Cont.)
    sliding, 24-25
    standing broad jump, 26
    throwing a small ball, 27
    walking, 27-28
    walking the beam, 28-29
  summary of, (table), 29-30
Movements, of locomotion, 7
Muscle sense, 3
Muscle spindles, 3
Myelinization, 4, 5

Nash, J.B., 101
National Association for the Education of Young Children, 95
Nerve-net, 34
Nervous system, 3, 4, 9, 32, 33
  autonomic, 5
  central, 5
  and physiological law of use, 2-4
Neurological development, 35
Neurological organization, 5
Neuromuscular complex, 34
Neuromuscular system, 7

Objective:
  of education, 7
  movement as, 7
Observing:
  general characteristics, 42
  help for, 11-12
  in prescriptive teaching, 60
  by teachers and parents, 99-100
  total body assembly, 45-46
Opposition, 8, 41
  and symmetry, 42, (table), 43
  use of equipment for, 88
Output, 34
Output system, 4, 5

Parent, 1
  parent-teacher relationship, 98
  sharing information, 98-99
  sharing responsibility, 99
Parental figure, 33
Patterning:
  passive, 34
  theory of, 34
Patterns:
  of fundamental movements, 12-30
  general characteristics of, 41-42
  of movement tasks, 12-30
  of related movements, 35-38
Perceptual control, 8
Perceptual experience, 8
  movement as, 2
Pestalozzi, Johann Heinrich, 5

Physical education, 97
  for young children, 97-108
Piaget, Jean, 5
Planning:
  day to day, 107
  long term, 107
  motor, 11
Porter, Lorena, 108
Postural adjustment, 49
Power, 36
  total body assembly for, 41,
    (table), 46
Prescribing, 61
Prescription, 63
Prescriptive teaching, 60-63
Program:
  assessment of, 101-2
    challenge in, 101
    effort in, 102
    joy in, 101
    novelty in, 101
    progress in, 102
    security in, 101-2
  in movement for young children, 99
  in physical education for young
    children, 99
Progress of children, 102
Proprioceptors, 3
  as a part of feedback mechanism, 5
Pulling, 23, 38
  likeness to pushing and carrying, 38
  persistence in, 38
  total body assembly in, 38
Pushing, 23, 38
  likeness to carrying and pulling, 38
  persistence in, 38
  total body assembly in, 38

Rappaport, Sheldon R., 60, 62
Rarick, G. Lawrence, 30
Readiness:
  for motor tasks, 7, 103
  for reading, 59
Reading readiness, related to developing
  movement, 59
Referrals, 100
Response, 6
  the child's, 33
  and interaction, 33
Rest, 104
Race, related to developing movement, 58
Rhythm, 8
Robertson, Mary Ann, 34
Running, 23-24
  space for, 80
Running high jump, 24
Russell, Joan, 108

Safety:
  in arranging space, 81
  in hitting, 90
  and readiness, 103
  in using slides and swings, 92
Sage, George H., 6
School:
  and the home, 98
  sharing information with, 98-99
  sharing responsibility with, 99
Scientific method of teaching, 63
Scores:
  children's interest in, 104
  as measures of time and distance,
    (table), 54
Seashore, H.G., 45
Security, 101-2
Self-discovery, 9, 10
Self-image, positive, 2
Self-patterning, 34
Sequence:
  in growth, 6
  of movement development, 1
  of movement patterns, 6
  proper, 9
  for teaching movement, 8
Sex, related to developing movement,
  55-58
Shoes, 84
"Show and tell," 107
Side-preference, (see Dominance)
Simpson, Dorothy M., 77
Sinclair, Caroline B., 6, 10, 30, 32, 34,
  40, 52, 64
Skipping, 24
  as related to the gallop and slide, 36
  in rhythmic two-part locomotion,
    46-47
Slides and swings, 92
Sliding, 24-25
  as related to the gallop and skip, 36
  in rhythmic two-part locomotion, 46-47
Smart, R.C., 2
Space, 79-82
  an essential for movement develop-
    ment, 32
  indoor, 80
  moving through, 36
  outdoor, 80
  stimulation provided by, 81-82
Spare parts, 4, 5
Speed, 37, 38
  in throwing and striking, 37
  total body assembly for, 41,
    (table), 46
Stairs:
  ascending, 12

Stairs, (Cont.)
  descending, 18
Standing, intermediate steps to, 6
Standing broad jump, 26-27
  landing from, 37, 91
  takeoff for, 36-37
Standing long jump, (see Standing broad jump)
Stimulus-response mechanism, 4
Strength, in total body assembly (see Force)
Stress factors, and physical exercise, 2
Striking, (see Hitting)
  and throwing, 37
Success in movement tasks, 12-30
Summary:
  of movement as education, 9-10
  of movement tasks (table), 29-30
  of what movement means to a child, 9-10
Surfacing:
  indoors, 83
  outdoors, 83
Swimming:
  facilities for, 82-83
  pattern of, 36
Swings and slides, 92
Symmetry, 8
  and opposition, 42, (table), 43
Synaptic association, 4
Synaptic efficiency, 5
Synchronous movement, 44
Synchrony, 8

Takeoff, for broad jump, 36-37
Task analysis, 61
Teacher:
  parent-teacher relationship, 98
  sharing information, 98-99
  sharing responsibility, 99
Teaching techniques, 103
  selection of, 61-62
Teachers:
  acceptance, 58, 103
  estimates of achievement, 60
  task, 39-40
Theory:
  of patterning, 34
  that movement supports other sensory functions, 9
Thompson, H., 6

Throwing:
  a small ball, 27
  and striking, 37
Time:
  for movement, 85-86
  amount of, 85-86
  indoors, 85
  outdoors, 85
  right for learning, 9
  system, inborn, 6
Tool subject:
  in learning, 7
  movement as, 7-9
Tool subjects, 2
Total body assembly, 37, 39, 41, 45-46
  for force, 41, 46
  for power, 41, 46
  for speed, 41, 46
  in throwing and striking, 37
Two-part movements, 35
  running, 23, 35-36
  skating, 36
  walking, 24, 35-36
Two-part rhythmic locomotion, 42, 46, (table), 47
Two-part rhythms, 36
  gallop, 19, 36
  skip, 24, 36
  slide, 24, 36

Underachiever, 2, 34
Understanding the child's response, 61
Unreadiness, 39

Vestibular organs, 3

Walking, 27-28
  intermediate steps to, 6
  postural adjustment in, 49
Walking beam:
  construction of, 110
  use of, 28-29
Walking the beam, 28-29
Water, 82-83
  for play, 82-83
  for swimming, 82-83
Weight transfer, 8
Whitehurst, Keturah E., 9, 10, 64
Wickstrom, Ralph L., 6, 40

Young, Norma Dorothy, 42